The Science of Reading Says

Literacy Strategies

for Early Childhood

Jodene L. Smith, M.A.

Shell Education

Contributing Authors

Erica Bowers, Ed.D.
Darcy Mellinger, M.A.
Hillary Wolfe, M.A.

Consultant

Jennifer Jump, M.A.

Publishing Credits

Corinne Burton, M.A.Ed., *President* and *Publisher*
Aubrie Nielsen, M.S.Ed., *EVP of Content Development*
Kyra Ostendorf, M.Ed., *Publisher, professional books*
Véronique Bos, *Vice President of Creative*
Cathy Hernandez, *Senior Content Manager*
Fabiola Sepulveda, *Junior Art Director*
Michelle Lee Lagerroos, *Interior Graphic Designer*
David Slayton, *Assistant Editor*

Image Credits

All images from iStock and/or Shutterstock.

A division of Teacher Created Materials
5482 Argosy Avenue
Huntington Beach, CA 92649-1039
www.tcmpub.com/shell-education
ISBN 978-1-0876-9672-0
© 2024 Shell Educational Publishing, Inc.
Printed in USA BRP001

Table of Contents

Introduction 1
   What the Science of Reading Says 1
   The Science of Reading: Models of Reading 2
   The Science of Reading: Implications for Teaching 4
   Components of Literacy 7
   Factors That Contribute to Success in Reading and Writing 10
   Differentiation 13
   Cultural Relevance 15
   How to Use This Book 17

Section I: Word Recognition 18
   What Is a Word? 30
   Working with Words—Compound Words 32
   Silly Willy Rhyming Words 38
   Create New Nursery Rhymes 40
   Feel the Syllables 42
   Making Sandwiches with Onsets and Rimes 44
   Isolating Sounds with Movement 48
   Sound Boxes 50
   Introducing Letters and Sounds 54
   Alphabet Sound Chart 56
   Working with an Alphabet Arc 59
   Alphabet Sorts 67
   Blending with Cruising Cars 78
   High-Frequency Word Match 82

Section II: Reading Comprehension and Content Knowledge 84
   Using Text Sets for Wide and Extensive Reading 95
   Creating Concept Maps 98
   What I Know 100
   Shared Experience 102
   Explicit Vocabulary Word Instruction 104
   Incidental Vocabulary Word Instruction 108
   Shades of Meaning 111
   Many Ways to Say It 113
   Identifying Multiple-Meaning Words 116
   Picture Inference 118

Figurative Language Awareness 121
Teaching Concepts of Print 123
Informational Text Genre Study 125

Section III: Writing 129
Print-Rich Environment 139
Multisensory Letter Formation Practice 141
Name Writing 143
Morning Message 145
Picture Word Chart 147
Experience, Talk, Write 149
Journal Writing 151
Predictable Sentences 155
The Big Three 158

References 160
Digital Resources 170

INTRODUCTION

What the Science of Reading Says

This book is one in a series of professional resources that provide teaching strategies aligned with the Science of Reading. The term *the Science of Reading* pervades the national conversation around the best literacy instruction for all students. The purpose of this series is to close the gap between the knowledge and understanding of what students need to become literate humans and the instructional practices in our schools. This gap is widely acknowledged yet remains intact. While research is available, journals are not easy to navigate. However, with concise resources that build understanding of the body of research and offer strategies aligned with that research, teachers can be equipped with the logical steps to find success. This book will help you navigate the important Science of Reading research and implement strategies based on that research in your classroom.

> The Science of Reading is the collection of research that leads to the understanding of how students learn to read.

What is meant by the phrase *Science of Reading*? The Science of Reading is the collection of research that leads to the understanding of how students learn to read. Research dedicated to understanding how we learn to read and write has been conducted for more than fifty years. This research has explored topics ranging from the skills needed to read and write, to the parts of the brain involved in reading development, to the best way to teach children how to read. The research clearly demonstrates the following: 1) the most effective early reading instruction includes an explicit, structured, phonics-based approach to word reading; and 2) reading comprehension relies on word reading (being able to decode individual words) and language comprehension (being able to understand what words and sentences mean).

According to the Report of the National Reading Panel (2000), a comprehensive program of literacy instruction should contain explicit skills instruction in phonemic awareness, phonics, fluency, vocabulary, and reading and language comprehension. Effective literacy instruction includes explicit instruction in all five of the components of reading plus writing. Ideally, this will occur in classrooms that emphasize and facilitate motivation for and engagement in reading through the use of a variety of authentic texts, authentic tasks, cooperative learning, and whole- and small-group instruction that connects reading to students' lived realities. Motivation and engagement are important considerations in our teaching. Cultural and linguistic relevance and responsiveness are essential. Authentic opportunities for speaking, listening, and writing are critical. Gradual release of responsibility is necessary to build independence and is an integral part of promoting a culture of literacy that students will embrace and take with them once they leave our care. Let us explore more closely what we can learn from the Science of Reading.

The Science of Reading: Models of Reading

The widely accepted model of the Simple View of Reading (SVR) proposed by Gough and Tunmer (1986) and later refined by Hoover and Gough (1990) depicts reading comprehension as the product of word recognition and language comprehension. This model of reading has had a significant impact on the field as it offered researchers and practitioners a simple, comprehensible way of organizing their thinking and understanding of the constructs that can predict successful literacy outcomes (Snow 2018). Hoover and Tunmer (2018) describe these constructs as:

- Word recognition: the ability to recognize printed words accurately and quickly to efficiently gain access to the appropriate word meanings contained in the internal mental lexicon.

- Language comprehension: the ability to extract and construct literal and inferred meaning from speech.

- Reading comprehension: the ability to extract and construct literal and inferred meaning from linguistic discourse represented in print.

Word Recognition
The ability to transform print into spoken language

×

Language Comprehension
The ability to understand spoken language

=

Reading Comprehension

The Simple View of Reading

Later work (Hoover and Tunmer 2020; Scarborough 2001) further describes the crucial elements within each of these constructs by incorporating the best of what science tells us about how we read. Scarborough's Reading Rope identifies the underlying skills required for effective and efficient word recognition and language comprehension.

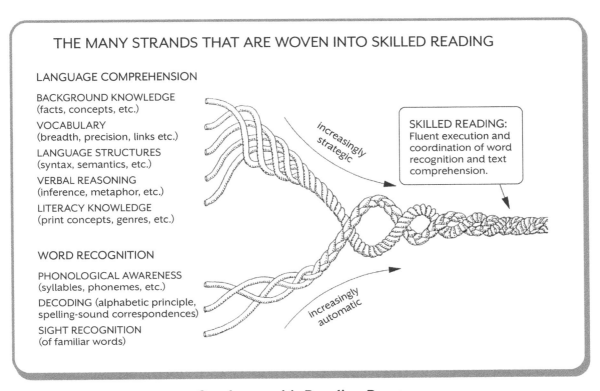

THE MANY STRANDS THAT ARE WOVEN INTO SKILLED READING

LANGUAGE COMPREHENSION

BACKGROUND KNOWLEDGE
(facts, concepts, etc.)
VOCABULARY
(breadth, precision, links etc.)
LANGUAGE STRUCTURES
(syntax, semantics, etc.)
VERBAL REASONING
(inference, metaphor, etc.)
LITERACY KNOWLEDGE
(print concepts, genres, etc.)

WORD RECOGNITION

PHONOLOGICAL AWARENESS
(syllables, phonemes, etc.)
DECODING (alphabetic principle,
spelling-sound correspondences)
SIGHT RECOGNITION
(of familiar words)

increasingly strategic

SKILLED READING:
Fluent execution and coordination of word recognition and text comprehension.

increasingly automatic

Scarborough's Reading Rope

Credit: Hollis Scarborough, "Connecting Early Language and Literacy to Later Reading (Dis)abilities: Evidence, Theory, and Practice" in *Handbook of Research in Early Literacy*, edited by Susan B. Neuman and David K. Dickinson © Guilford Press, 2001.

Wesley Hoover, William Tunmer, Philip Gough, and Hollis Scarborough are psychologists who dedicated their research to understanding what reading is and what must be present or learned for reading to occur. They describe the SVR as simple because it is intended to focus our attention on what is important in reading but *not* to explain the process of *how* reading happens. Similarly, Scarborough expanded on the SVR to focus attention on more specific details of language comprehension and word recognition such as prior knowledge and phonological awareness, attempting to include space for process with the addition of automaticity and strategy. Both the SVR and the Reading Rope are models—hypotheses that attempt to explain the phenomena of reading. The models describe necessary but not sufficient conditions for reading. Many teachers know that decoding skills can be present, language comprehension can be apparent, and yet comprehension can be impeded. These foundational models do not account for motivation, development, social-emotional considerations, linguistic differences, and a host of other factors relevant to literacy teaching and learning.

In the use and understanding of these models, one can see how the Science of Reading brings together expertise across disciplines. This model of skilled reading provides literacy researchers and classroom educators with a roadmap for the development of instructional practices that promote these essential skills.

The Science of Reading: Implications for Teaching

Here is where we are wise to remember the Science of Reading relies on the *sciences* of reading. It encompasses many fields. The modeling work of cognitive and educational psychologists informs the work of others in literacy research. The work of the literacy researchers informs the work of those who translate it into instructional practices. The end goal is to explain the processes by which successful reading occurs and the most effective ways to develop skills that enable these processes. As Louisa Moats declared, *teaching reading is rocket science!* In this seminal piece, Moats describes how teachers can think about the Simple View of Reading in relation to their classroom practice:

> The implications of the Simple View of Reading should be self-evident: reading and language arts instruction must include deliberate, systematic, and explicit teaching of word recognition and must develop students' subject-matter knowledge, vocabulary, sentence comprehension, and familiarity with the language in written texts. Each of these larger skill domains depends on the integrity of its subskills. (Moats 2020a, para. 11)

Moats's description reflects the recommendations of the National Reading Panel (NRP) (2000) and the modeling by the cognitive scientists. The evidence base from the sciences informing our understanding of reading consistently supports systematic and direct instruction in the five components of reading: phonemic awareness, phonics, fluency, vocabulary, and comprehension.

Phonological Awareness and Phonemic Awareness

Phonological awareness is an umbrella term that refers to noticing and manipulating sounds in speech, for instance, individual words, syllables, and sounds in words. Pre-readers who have phonological awareness skills recognize rhymes and alliterative sounds in chants, songs, and picture books. These activities set the stage for students to navigate how speech sounds relate to both spoken and printed words. *Phonemic awareness*, a subcategory of phonological awareness, is the understanding that spoken words are made of individual sounds called *phonemes*. Research demonstrates that phonemic awareness can be taught and that this teaching is effective for a variety of learners (NRP 2000; National Early Literacy Panel 2008). It assists children in learning to read and learning to spell. Explicitly teaching children to manipulate phonemes, focused on one or two types of phoneme manipulations rather than multiple types, and teaching children in small groups are most effective (NRP 2000). According to the recommendations of the NRP report, children should receive approximately 18 hours (about 6 minutes a day for 180 days) of phonemic awareness instruction to learn these skills. Phonemic awareness instruction is crucial in kindergarten and should occur in grades 1 and 2 as needed.

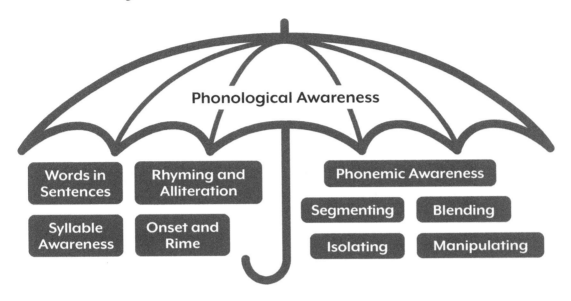

Phonics

Phonics is the term used to describe the relationships between the letters (*graphemes*) of written language and the individual sounds (*phonemes*) of spoken language. Phonics instruction helps children learn and use the alphabetic principle—the understanding that there are systematic and predictable relationships between written letters and spoken sounds (Armbruster, Lehr, and Osborn 2010). Children need knowledge of phonics to become efficient, automatic decoders of written text. Explicit, systematic instruction in phonics has been shown to be most effective, regardless of the approach used (NRP 2000). There are three approaches to teaching phonics: (1) *synthetic phonics*, which emphasizes teaching students to convert letters into sounds and then to blend sounds to form words; (2) *analytic phonics*, during which children do not pronounce sounds in isolation but rather learn to analyze letter-sound relationships in previously learned words; (3) *analogy-based phonics*, in which children learn to use parts of word families they know to recognize new unknown words that may contain the same parts. Most important is that phonics instruction is systematic and explicit. While not all children need intensive phonics instruction, no student is harmed by or will have their reading progress impeded by receiving phonics instruction. Many students will benefit significantly from systematic phonics instruction in grades K through 2.

> Children need knowledge of phonics to become efficient, automatic decoders of written text. Explicit, systematic instruction in phonics has been shown to be most effective.

Fluency

Fluency is defined as the ability to read with speed, accuracy, and proper expression. It is a critical component of skilled reading. Fluency depends upon well-developed word recognition skills readers can apply to silent reading or reading aloud that make word reading rapid, accurate, and cognitively efficient. When children are fluent readers they spend less time trying to decode or pronounce words and can better attend to the comprehension of text. However, fluency also represents a level of expertise beyond word recognition accuracy (NRP 2000). Phrasing, intonation, and monitoring reading are all considered fluency skills. Research demonstrates that students benefit from fluency instruction and that reading comprehension may be aided by fluency (NRP 2000). For young learners, fluency is modeled by media and by fluent readers in their lives, including family members and teachers.

Vocabulary

Vocabulary refers to the words we must understand to communicate effectively. Vocabulary plays an important role in reading comprehension. Children who develop strong vocabularies and continue to deepen and broaden their vocabulary knowledge find it easier to comprehend more of what they read, especially as text becomes more complex (Sinatra, Zygouris-Coe, and Dasinger 2012). Moreover, students who have strong vocabularies have less difficulty learning unfamiliar words because those words are likely to be related to words that students already know (Rupley, Logan, and Nichols 1999). Researchers and educators often refer to and consider four types of vocabulary: *listening vocabulary* consists of the words we need to know to understand what we hear; *speaking vocabulary* consists of words we use to speak; *reading vocabulary* refers to the words we need to understand what we read; and *writing vocabulary* is the words we use in writing (Armbruster, Lehr, and Osborn 2010).

> Children who develop strong vocabularies and continue to deepen and broaden their vocabulary knowledge find it easier to comprehend more of what they read.

Research reveals that most vocabulary is learned indirectly, but some must be taught directly (Armbruster, Lehr, and Osborn 2010). Vocabulary instruction should be direct and explicit.

Comprehension

Research repeatedly demonstrates that students benefit greatly from direct, explicit instruction in reading comprehension strategies and instruction in other areas that support reading comprehension (Duke and Pearson 2002; Duke, Ward, and Pearson 2021; Durkin 1978; Pressley and Afflerbach 1995). The NRP (2000) identified a number of effective strategies for teaching comprehension. These strategies include vocabulary development, prediction skills (including inferencing), the building of a broad base of topical knowledge, the activation of prior knowledge, think-alouds, visual representations, summarization, and questioning. Students also need to develop their metacognitive skills to become strategic and independent readers. Most literacy researchers agree that metacognition plays a significant role in reading comprehension (Baker and Brown 1984; Gourgey 1998; Hacker, Dunlosky, and Graesser 1998; Palincsar and Brown 1987). Research shows that teachers should foster metacognition and comprehension monitoring during comprehension instruction because in doing so, students will learn to monitor and self-regulate their ability to read.

Throughout this book, we delve more deeply into each of these areas to share and explain the research as it applies to specific areas of reading development and to students of different grade levels.

Components of Literacy

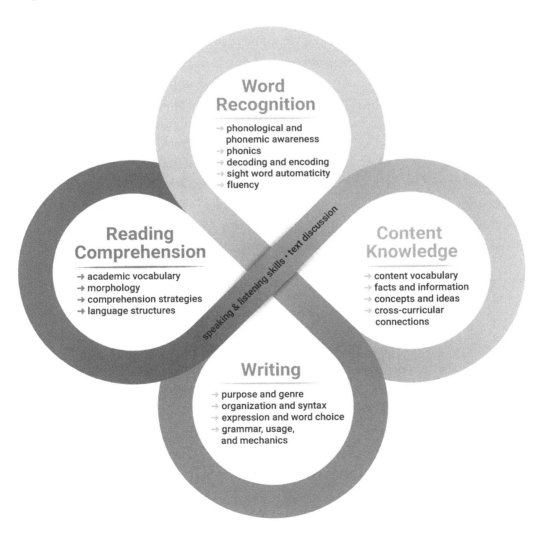

The figure on page 7 reflects what we know to be essential components of comprehensive literacy instruction. This visual representation of the Science of Reading brings together what we know from multiple sciences of literacy, from research in early literacy, from research on the reading-writing connection, from the national reports on reading and literacy, and from the cognitive sciences. Development of skills in word recognition, comprehension, content knowledge, and writing are well supported in the research as effective practices for literacy instruction. The figure includes the five components of reading recommended by the NRP, however the reorganization of these components into the four constructs is intentional and represents the evolution in understanding the connections between reading and the wider consideration of what it means to be literate. Just as the SVR was intended to call our attention to the components of reading comprehension (Hoover and Tunmer 2022), the subcategories describing each component of this model give us guidance as to where to focus our teaching in order to support skilled reading and literacy development.

The inclusion of content knowledge as a separate construct is important in this model. Research has long struggled over the role of content knowledge in reading comprehension. We are well aware of the fact that the activation and development of prior knowledge (schema) is important to comprehension; we know that knowledge of words and word parts plays a key role in the decoding of new and/or unfamiliar words and determining the meaning of such words. Of primary importance for activating prior knowledge is the presence of relevant knowledge. There is a growing body of research that demonstrates the critical role of content knowledge in comprehension of text concerning that topic. In fact, the knowledge a reader brings (content and word knowledge) is the primary determinant of comprehension (Anderson and Pearson 1984; Cabell and Hwang 2020). Content knowledge can support readers in making inferences and connections to text. This can deepen understanding of a text and support learning as readers are better able to connect what they read in text to existing schema

> There is a growing body of research that demonstrates the critical role of content knowledge in comprehension of text concerning that topic.

in ways that develop new learning (Cabell and Hwang 2020). Cabell and Hwang's (2020) recent review of the "relatively small but robust" body of research on content-rich literacy instruction demonstrates its important role in developing language and knowledge in support of reading comprehension. The inclusion of content knowledge as a separate and co-important construct in this model also serves as an important reminder that the Science of Reading goes beyond the narrow discussion of skills-based decoding instruction and that our literacy instruction should be embedded in meaningful context.

Including writing as a component in the model draws attention to the important role writing plays in literacy development and the reciprocal relationship writing shares with reading. Decades of research demonstrate that direct and explicit teaching of writing skills, strategies, and processes is effective at improving students' writing and communication skills (Graham et al. 2012). There is much to be gained from bringing reading and writing study and practice together (Graham 2020). Reading and writing draw from a shared set of literacy knowledge and skills, including vocabulary development, background knowledge, and an understanding of syntax, semantics, and morphology. Additionally, reading across genres to understand how one communicates in a particular genre can inform writing in that genre. Writing in response to reading makes comprehension "visible" as students summarize, explain, infer, and make connections to what they have read.

Finally, wrapping the components of this literacy model in a "ribbon" of speaking and listening serves as a powerful reminder that speaking and listening are essential to literacy development. Though reading and writing are not natural processes, our brains are hardwired for communicating through speaking and listening (Hulit, Howard, and Fahey 2018). Researchers and experienced educators can attest to the fact that listening comprehension skills and oral language abilities are generally more developed than students' reading and writing skills, particularly in younger children (Sticht and James 1984). Drawing on the stronger listening comprehension skills of young readers can enhance vocabulary development, build knowledge of complex language structures, and aid content knowledge as students can comprehend through listening what they would not be able to read. Larger vocabularies and broad content knowledge in turn support reading comprehension and writing skills. As students' reading and writing skills progress, it is important that speaking and listening skills do the same. Speaking is directly connected to our thinking and learning. Opportunities to talk to others about our thoughts require us to be active in our thinking, making decisions about how to explain understanding and reflect and analyze what we know or may not know. These conversations and discussions can help students make sense of new information and construct new meaning (Barnes and Todd 1995; Halliday 1975). Speaking and listening support the development of all other literacy skills, including reading comprehension and writing, and must be an essential element of effective literacy instruction.

> Speaking and listening support the development of all other literacy skills, including reading comprehension and writing, and must be an essential element of effective literacy instruction.

Factors That Contribute to Success in Reading and Writing

As mentioned above, success in reading and writing can be influenced by more than just explicit instruction in the components of literacy. Duke and Cartwright's (2021) Active View of Reading points to important factors that impact students, including cultural knowledge, motivation and engagement, and executive functioning skills. Each of these can be a determiner of student success. As well as addressing the needs of those students who are progressing at different rates, differentiation is essential for providing all students with the necessary tools for success. Many students enter our classrooms speaking a language other than English and need extra support while attaining English language proficiency. Below is a discussion of how teachers can create a supportive classroom environment and address these additional factors.

Motivating Students to Read

Ensuring that students are interested and engaged in the work of reading is one aspect of instruction that cannot be overlooked. Teachers must identify a range of ways to both engage and motivate their students.

> Ensuring that students have access to a wide range of texts will help each student find something to be passionate about.

INTERESTS

To foster a lifelong love for reading and writing that extends beyond the day-to-day literacy tasks of classroom life, teachers should become familiar with students' interests as early in the school year as possible with the goal of providing students with reading materials and writing assignments that are tailored to their interests, passions, and wonderings. Ensuring that students have access to a wide range of texts will help each student find something to be passionate about. Providing suggestions rather than rules about the types of texts to read allows for students to choose books that are informational, or contain poetry, or fables, or stories. Once these high-interest texts and assignments are made available, students are more likely to be self-motivated to read and write because they want to discover and share more about the topics that interest them. This self-motivated act of reading and writing develops students' desire to learn that is so important in accessing content from a wide range of texts and text types beyond their interests. Reading and writing about texts of interest allows students to fine-tune their skills in the context of experiences that are interesting, familiar, and comfortable for them, in turn providing them with the confidence and practice needed to effectively navigate texts that are more advanced, unfamiliar, or unexciting.

AUTHENTIC OPPORTUNITIES

There are several ways to offer authentic opportunities for children to purposefully engage with interesting texts. Challenge students to use reading to find their names, recognize words, identify where to find classroom supplies, understand rules and procedures, or follow directions for a recipe or game. Reading challenges such as these can be formulated and scripted by the teacher, or they can be generic and allow for students to both create the pathway and discover the journey. For example, if a group of young learners shows interest in learning more about silk moths after a science lesson, provide a text set for them to engage with. Allow for students to choose which texts to read, which pathway to follow, and how they will share what they have learned. Similarly, if a group of third graders shows interest in a character, put together a bin of texts with similar characters. Provide students with the challenge: discover who is most interesting and prove it. These types of opportunities increase student time spent reading and writing. Without motivation, students will spend less time reading and writing, providing less opportunity to perfect literacy skills, build knowledge, and develop wide vocabulary.

OUTSIDE READING

In addition to discovering students' interests and providing suggestions and texts based on your findings, one of the easiest and most effective ways to improve reading comprehension and writing ability is to promote extensive reading outside of class. Students who frequently read a wide variety of materials have better vocabularies and better reading comprehension skills. They also can use those texts as models for future writing. As Randall Ryder and Michael Graves (2003) point out, wide reading fosters automaticity in students because it exposes them to more words in different contexts, provides them with knowledge on a variety of topics, and promotes lifelong reading habits.

A teacher's attitude toward reading and writing, especially for pleasure outside of school, has a tremendous effect on the students in the classroom. Teachers who talk enthusiastically about books they have read and who model reading and writing as an enjoyable and fulfilling experience foster a love for reading and writing in their students. Teachers who can recommend books that are particularly engaging and interesting can increase student motivation tremendously. Teachers should have an intimate knowledge of reading materials for a wide range of abilities so they can recommend books to any student to read outside of class.

> Teachers who talk enthusiastically about books they have read and who model reading and writing as enjoyable, fulfilling experiences foster a love for reading and writing in their students.

THE CLASSROOM LIBRARY

A powerful step is to set up a classroom library. Why is it important to have a classroom library? According to Lesley Mandel Morrow (2003), children in classrooms with book collections read 50 percent more books than children in classrooms without such collections.

Teachers can collaborate with the school librarian or media specialist and parent organizations to build a sizeable collection of texts for their classrooms, which should be a mixture of informational and fictional books. Bear in mind that this library may serve to generate the interest to read a variety of texts on many different subjects, so providing students with a wide range of texts from which to choose will be beneficial in fostering students' desire and motivation to read and write. In addition to simply providing students with informational and fictional texts, be sure to provide texts that are at your students' readiness levels and also texts that may present more of a challenge. Especially with interest-based texts, students can build their prior knowledge about a given topic at a less challenging reading level, preparing them to apply a variety of reading strategies to navigate more advanced texts on the same topic. Michael Pressley and his colleagues (2003) found that high-motivation and high-performing classrooms were, above all, filled with books at different levels of text difficulty.

The reading materials should be housed in bookcases that provide easy access for students to browse and choose books. Use tubs to hold magazines and articles on related topics and themes. Students will be better able to discover the power of books and other texts if the materials are purposefully organized: science, science fiction, history, historical fiction, mystery, fantasy, adventure, poetry, and other types of literature. Once the materials are in place, incorporate them into your instruction. Read to students every day! Dedicate time to supporting students in navigating the books, and encourage wide reading by making independent reading and exploration of books a regular classroom activity.

> While we can entice students with carefully crafted libraries, success may still be hindered if we neglect to address their individual needs.

Motivation is one factor that impacts the successful development of reading and writing ability. While we can entice students with carefully crafted libraries, success may still be hindered if we neglect to address their individual needs. This means meeting students where they are and providing appropriate instruction and support, whether they are an English learner, striving reader, or accelerated learner.

Differentiation

As teachers, we know that students come into our classrooms at varying reading, writing, and readiness levels to access the content at hand. The strategies in this book offer suggestions for differentiating for different groups of students so that they can benefit from the strategy being implemented, whether those groups are English learners, striving (below grade level) students, or accelerated (above grade level) students. All students in our classrooms deserve access to rich and rigorous content. Differentiating the content, the process, the product, and the environment allows for all students to find success in learning to read and write.

Our goal is to help students acquire proficiency in reading and writing. As part of this goal, it is our responsibility to provide students with meaningful and interesting contexts to learn language and build their reading and writing skills. In doing so, teachers simultaneously aid in the development of students' collaborative, communicative, and group-based skills emphasized in speaking and listening standards, subsequently helping all students to strategically communicate and interact with those around them within the context of the English language.

> Differentiating the content, the process, the product, and the environment allows for all students to find success in learning to read and write.

English Learners

When implementing the strategies in this book, provide English learners with ample opportunities to talk with their classmates and adults to develop language. The development of oral language skills sets the framework for developing literacy skills. These opportunities must be intentional and designed to support literacy learning. Develop a classroom space that allows students to feel safe and secure so learning can occur. It is important to note that providing English learners with scaffolds for accessing content, developing early literacy skills, and engaging with the context of unfamiliar cultural references that native English speakers are naturally more familiar with builds pathways for all students to find success. Giving English learners access to foundational skills that will help develop their overall reading ability is also essential to developing their writing skills. Ample opportunities to engage with rich content supports multilingual students in developing the knowledge and vocabulary that underpins their understanding. In addition, English learners "will benefit from actively seeking exposure to language and social interaction with others who can provide meaningful input in the second language. Furthermore, they—and you, the teacher—can enhance students' English language skills by placing language learning in meaningful and interesting contexts" (Dunlap and Weisman 2006, 11).

Striving Learners

In addition to building motivation through interest-based texts, striving students will benefit from scaffolding. While all students benefit from explicit, authentic instruction, these are crucial elements for striving readers. Striving readers can benefit from participating in a small group before the whole-class lesson to have the opportunity to learn the information in a lower-risk environment, with text at a developmentally appropriate level. They may also need further practice with the content after instruction. It is vital that striving learners are provided with additional scaffolds to ensure their success.

Accelerated Learners

While it is critical to differentiate lessons for the striving learner, accelerated students also benefit from modifications to instruction. Teachers can challenge accelerated learners by extending the content either in depth or breadth (Tomlinson 2014). In addition, teachers can provide accelerated learners with opportunities to demonstrate their understanding of content by modifying the process (how students are provided the content) or the product (what students produce to demonstrate understanding). Adapting curriculum for accelerated learners also addresses issues of motivation, as providing tasks that are cognitively challenging maintains their interest.

Flexible Grouping

Throughout this text we recommend ways to differentiate the lessons to better accommodate all students. Some modalities we recommend are whole class, small groups, collaborative learning, and partner pairs.

Whole class may be used for:

- introducing a new strategy or concept
- modeling think-alouds to show students how to use the strategy
- practicing think-alouds and allowing students to share their experiences and ideas using the strategy

Small groups may be used for:

- pre-teaching new strategies, concepts, and vocabulary
- providing more intensive instruction for striving students
- checking students' understanding of how to apply strategies to the text they are reading or composing
- introducing accelerated students to a strategy so that they can apply it independently to more challenging texts

- encouraging students to use a strategy to think more deeply than they might have imagined possible

Collaborative learning may be used for:

- allowing students to practice strategies without teacher involvement (the teacher is available and "walking the room" to monitor student progress and understanding)
- providing striving students with peer support in completing tasks

Pair students with partners to:

- share responses and ideas when trying out strategies

Cultural Relevance

Students learn best when they feel they can take risks and be open to new experiences. For this to happen, teachers need to create spaces where everyone feels valued and that they belong. One way to do this is to design a classroom that represents the diverse backgrounds and cultures of our students. Being mindful of students' home lives, cultures, and language experiences is known as being culturally and linguistically responsive. According to Sharroky Hollie, cultural and linguistic responsiveness (CLR) can be defined as the "validation and affirmation of the home (indigenous) culture and home language for the purposes of building and bridging the student to success in the culture of academia and mainstream society" (2018, 23).

Being a culturally and linguistically responsive educator is a journey. The concepts may be well-known, or they may be new. Culturally and linguistically responsive educators are self-aware and socially aware. They are aware of their own cultural backgrounds, which includes ethnicity, nationality, religion, age, and gender, among other things. In the classroom, culturally and linguistically responsive educators are responsive to cultural differences and have an unconditional positive regard for students and their cultures. They strive to continually learn about students and their cultures, adjusting their perspectives and practices to best serve students.

Culturally and linguistically responsive classrooms are print-rich and display the linguistic supports multilingual learners and others need to be successful. This includes the academic vocabulary that students are learning, which they need to access to be able to discuss language and content. In addition, these classrooms are active. Students utilize the four language components and are engaged in discussions with peers and teachers. They are

> In the classroom, culturally and linguistically responsive educators are sensitive to cultural differences and have an unconditional positive regard for students and their cultures.

physically active and move around the room to work with peers on a variety of projects. The materials being utilized reflect a variety of cultures and perspectives, and student work is prominently displayed and honored.

Culturally and linguistically responsive educators design curriculum by selecting texts with characters and pictures that represent their students. They create shared writing pieces that draw from the students' home languages and cultures. They encourage students to research areas of interest and produce art that validates and exhibits their cultures. Culturally and linguistically responsive educators are constantly reevaluating their curricular choices to ensure all students are represented and validated.

> Culturally and linguistically responsive educators design curriculum by selecting texts with characters and pictures that represent their students.

Hollie (2018) embraces a philosophy of affirming students' home cultures and languages and suggests educators "love outrageously." To be culturally and linguistically responsive, educators must know their students. When educators validate students' cultures and languages through classroom management and materials, they help students see themselves reflected in the curriculum and allow students to use their backgrounds to supplement the classroom learning environment.

Taking a culturally and linguistically responsive stance is a holistic approach. It embraces the whole learner. When students feel they belong, are validated, and are represented in the curriculum, they are open and connected to the learning. Teaching in this manner allows for everyone's story to be told.

How to Use This Book

This book includes a variety of strategies that can be integrated into any language arts curriculum to teach reading and writing concepts and skills: print concepts, phonological awareness, the alphabetic principle, word recognition, decoding and encoding, sight recognition, vocabulary development, language structures, text genres, purpose and mechanics of writing, and using writing to convey meaning. These research-based instructional strategies will help teachers bridge the gap between the science of literacy instruction and classroom practice.

The strategies are presented in three sections: I) Word Recognition; II) Reading Comprehension and Content Knowledge; and III) Writing. These three sections correspond with three professional resources: *What the Science of Reading Says about Word Recognition* (Jump and Johnson 2023), *What the Science of Reading Says about Comprehension and Content Knowledge* (Jump and Kopp 2023), and *What the Science of Reading Says about Writing* (Jump and Wolfe 2023).

Each section opens with an overview of research in that area to emphasize the importance of that particular component. There is a clear and detailed explanation of the component, suggestions for instruction, and best practices. This information provides teachers with the solid foundation of knowledge to provide deeper, more meaningful instruction to their students.

Following each overview are a variety of instructional strategies. The strategies in the book include the following:

- background information that includes a description and purpose of the strategy
- the objective of the strategy
- a detailed description of how to implement the strategy, including any special preparation that might be needed
- suggestions for differentiating instruction

When applicable, the strategy includes reproducible materials in this book and in the digital resources. Examples of how the strategy is applied are also included when applicable. For more information about the digital resources, see page 170.

Word Recognition

The strategies in this section correspond with key competencies identified in *What the Science of Reading Says about Word Recognition* (Jump and Johnson 2023). These research-based instructional strategies will help teachers bridge the gap between the science of literacy instruction and classroom practice.

Strategy	Skills and Understandings Addressed		
	Phonological Awareness	Phonics	Sight Recognition
What Is a Word?			
Working with Words—Compound Words			
Silly Willy Rhyming Words			
Create New Nursery Rhymes			
Feel the Syllables			
Making Sandwiches with Onsets and Rimes			
Isolating Sounds with Movement			
Sound Boxes			

Strategy	Skills and Understandings Addressed		
	Phonological Awareness	Phonics	Sight Recognition
Introducing Letters and Sounds			
Alphabet Sound Chart			
Working with an Alphabet Arc			
Alphabet Sorts			
Blending with Cruising Cars			
High-Frequency Word Match			

The Foundations of Literacy and Word Recognition

Before children even enter a classroom, they begin to build aspects of literacy they will use on the road to becoming lifelong readers. Most children are exposed to language in a variety of ways, including conversations with adults, symbols on street signs, labels on products, keystrokes on tablets or phones, newspaper headlines, story time picture books at the library or at bedtime . . . and the list goes on. Prekindergarten and kindergarten teachers continue this exposure in our classrooms. Introducing children to the concept of reading and ensuring they understand that spoken words are represented by symbols prepares them for instruction in word recognition. Providing print-rich environments and safe spaces where children can take risks with language is also critical to their continued growth. A strong foundation in literacy is essential for children to blossom into skilled readers and writers.

Foundational literacy skills include concepts of print (print carries meaning), phonological awareness (manipulating units of oral language), and the alphabetic principle (understanding that letters represent sounds). Explicit instruction in these elements is crucial for learners in prekindergarten and kindergarten.

Concepts of Print

Concepts of print, or print awareness, means children understand that print can be used to deliver different types of information. They begin to understand that store signs carry meaning (*logographics*, e.g., realizing the golden arches represent McDonalds). Children start to understand that words and pictures serve as symbols at a very young age. Research suggests that "by 15 months of age . . . when pictures are labeled, both the word and the picture are taken as symbols for real world entities" (Ganea et al. 2009, 295). When students have print awareness, they also understand how to hold a book, which way to turn the pages, and, nowadays, which direction to swipe on a tablet or device to go from beginning to end. They also understand that letters are put together to create words and that spaces come between words to form sentences. In a larger sense, they understand that a book can tell a story, a gaming guide explains how to play, and typing words into an internet browser can produce an answer to a question.

> As emergent readers gain an understanding of concepts of print, they are ready for instruction in phonological awareness.

For students to gain print awareness, they need to be surrounded by print and to see adults modeling how to use print to gain information. At a grocery store, adults can point out the sign by the apples that shows how much they cost per pound. When teachers share texts, they can point to the title, show where the author's name is, put their finger under each word as they read, and show how to turn pages to go from the front of the book to the back. As emergent readers gain an understanding of concepts of print, they are ready for instruction in phonological awareness.

Phonological and Phonemic Awareness

Phonological awareness is the ability to identify and orally manipulate words and sounds. Research shows that phonological awareness is essential for the development of reading because of the relationship between the spoken word and the written word and that phonological awareness of the sounds of spoken language is required to learn letter-sound correspondence (Ehri et al. 2001; Kilpatrick 2015, 2016; Moats 2020b; Yopp and Yopp 2022). Phonological awareness is understanding that there are breaks in sound between words in a sentence, recognizing syllables within a word, and separating the sounds in a word to determine beginning, medial, and ending sounds. Instruction in phonological awareness should include the manipulation and detection of sounds, from larger parts to smaller parts. Prekindergarten and kindergarten teachers can have children identify larger chunks of sound, like words within compound words and syllables, to smaller parts, like onsets and rimes, where the /k/ in *cat* is the onset and /ăt/ is the rime. Children can play with rhyme and alliteration (e.g., *The boat can float in the moat*, or *Annie ate apples at Abigail's*).

> Research shows that phonological awareness is essential for the development of reading because of the relationship between the spoken word and the written word.

For readers to move to the word recognition stage, it is crucial for them to gain a strong foundation in phonemic awareness (Adams 2011; Ehri 2014, 2020; Ehri et al. 2001). *Phonemic awareness* is under the umbrella of phonological awareness, and specifically relates to manipulating the individual sounds in a word (see figure on page 5). While there are twenty-six letters in the English language, there are about forty-four phonemes because some sounds are represented by more than one letter, e.g., /sh/. Children can be introduced to phonemic awareness through activities that isolate sounds while showing the letter correspondence (/p/ in *paste*). Teachers can start to connect letters to the sounds they make, categorize letters and sounds, or remove letters from a word and ask children to identify how the sound of the word changes. Using rhyme and alliteration through chants and songs, orally tapping out syllables in words, manipulating onsets and rimes (*cat, mat, sat, hat*), and identifying and matching initial, medial, and final sounds (Which picture begins with /s/? Which ends in /s/?) are all activities that support phonemic awareness.

The Alphabetic Principle

Another foundational skill children need to ensure success with literacy is the ability to recognize that in the English language, letters and symbols represent speech sounds. Children learn that letters represent sounds, or, to use academic language, that *graphemes*

> Ensuring that early readers have a strong understanding of the alphabetic principle supports building their word recognition skills.

represent *phonemes*. Grasping the alphabetic principle assists with *orthographic mapping* wherein readers use the spelling, pronunciation, and meaning of words to form a mental image that they can quickly retrieve (Ehri 2005a, 2017). In the English language, matching sounds to letters is made more difficult due to the integration of spellings that represent sounds from Old and Middle English along with other languages (e.g., the words *my* [Middle English], *you* [Germanic], *said* [Arabic], *come* [Middle English], and *what* [Old English]). Because of these variations, teachers must be explicit when teaching some English spellings, being aware of the sound children hear, and calling out inconsistencies in spelling patterns. Ensuring that early readers have a strong understanding of the alphabetic principle supports building their word recognition skills.

Phases of Word Recognition

It can be helpful to turn to Ehri's (1987; 1992; 2005; 2020) phases of word reading to better understand the development of word recognition skills. Ehri describes four overlapping phases of word reading that students move through as they learn to read (decode) and spell (encode). Each phase is labeled to reflect and describe the type of knowledge applied during it to read and spell words: pre-alphabetic, partial alphabetic, full alphabetic, and consolidated alphabetic (Ehri 1987; 1992; 1998; 2020). The chart on the next page summarizes readers' skills in each phase.

Phase of Word Reading	Skills
Pre-Alphabetic	Early readers apply visual, nonalphabetic cues to read words. For example, remembering the "two round eyes" for the *oo* in *look* (Ehri 1998), the tail at the end of *dog*, or the hump in the middle of *camel* (Gough, Juel, and Roper-Schneider 1983).
Partial Alphabetic	Learners apply beginning knowledge of letter-sound correspondence to reading words, often focusing on the initial and the final consonants. For example, remembering /s/ and /n/ to read *spoon* (Ehri 1998). Readers often combine this knowledge with context clues to recognize words. They are often better able to recognize the words in context than in isolation.
Full Alphabetic	Readers have a well-developed knowledge of letter-sound correspondence. They use decoding skills to analyze letter-sound connections within words to read and spell them from memory (Ehri 2020).
Consolidated Alphabetic	Learners consolidate letter patterns into larger patterns that represent syllables and morphemes, have stored these in memory, and can apply them to decode and make connections to multisyllabic words (Ehri 2020).

The Pre-Alphabetic Stage: Phonological and Phonemic Awareness

At the pre-alphabetic stage, both phonological and phonemic awareness rely completely on oral language and the detection of sounds. Phonological awareness is broader than phonemic awareness and includes manipulating units of oral language, for instance, identifying individual words in a sentence, separating syllables in a word, separating the sounds in a word, and determining beginning, medial, and ending sounds in a word.

Phonemic awareness specifically relates to manipulating the sounds in an individual word. The figure on page 24 provides a list of phonemes. Adams (2011, 14) shares six tasks recommended by the NRP (2000) in building phonemic awareness:

1. Phoneme isolation: "Tell me the first sound in the word *paste*." (/p/)

2. Phoneme identity: "Tell me the sound that is the same in the words *bike*, *boy*, and *bell*." (/b/)

3. Phoneme categorization: "Which word does not belong: *bus*, *bun*, or *rug*?" (*rug*)

4. Phoneme blending: "What word is /s/ /t/ /ŏ/ /p/?" (*stop*)

5. Phoneme segmentation: "How many sounds are there in *ship*?" (three: /sh/ /ĭ/ /p/)

6. Phoneme deletion: "What word is *smile* without the /s/?" (*mile*)

Recognized Phonemes

Symbol	Sound
/ā/	angel, rain
/ă/	cat, apple
/ē/	eat, seed
/ĕ/	echo, red
/ī/	island, light
/ĭ/	in, sit
/ō/	oatmeal, bone
/ŏ/	octopus, mom
/ŭ/	up, hum
/o͞o/	oodles, moon
/o͝o/	put, book
/ə/	above, sofa
/oi/, /oy/	oil, boy
/ou/, /ow/	out, cow
/aw/, /ô/	awful, caught
/är/	car, far
/ôr/	four, or
/ûr/	her, bird, turn
/b/	baby, crib
/k/	cup, stick
/d/	dog, end
/f/	phone, golf

Symbol	Sound
/g/	gift, dog
/h/	happy, hat
/j/	jump, bridge
/l/	lip, fall
/m/	mother, home
/n/	nose, on
/p/	pencil, pop
/r/	rain, care
/s/	soup, face
/t/	time, cat
/v/	vine, of
/wh/	what, why
/w/	wet, wind
/y/	yes, beyond
/z/	zoo, because
/th/	thing, health
/th/	this, brother
/sh/	shout, machine
/zh/	pleasure, vision
/ch/	children, scratch
/ng/	ring, finger

Source: Hallie Kay Yopp and Ruth Helen Yopp, *Purposeful Play for Early Childhood Phonological Awareness*, 2nd edition. © Shell Education, 2022. Used with permission.

The Partial Alphabetic Phase: The Alphabetic Principle and Word Recognition

While phonemic awareness is the ability to hear and manipulate distinct sounds in words, the alphabetic principle is the understanding that letters represent those sounds and form the basis for word recognition. Once students have a strong footing in phonemics, they will be ready to transition from *auditory discrimination* (identifying different sounds) to *visual discrimination* (identifying different letters). Prekindergarten teachers can introduce the concept that sounds are represented by letters and those letters have names; at the partial-alphabetic stage teachers will want to explicitly teach these letter/sound relationships. Understanding the alphabetic principle and making the letter-sound connection prepares children for instruction in word recognition.

> Research recommends a letter-a-day approach rather than a letter-a-week approach, with each lesson lasting no more than 15 minutes (Reutzel 2015).

There is no agreed-upon order to introduce individual letters, but there is agreement that instruction should focus on letters that have the highest utility or can be used to make the most words. Introduce consonants that can be combined with vowels to make the most two- to three-letter words (e.g., *at, mat, bat*). Effective instruction includes the introduction of one or two consonants with a short vowel. (With the exception of a few long *e*, two-letter words (*be, me, he, we*), short vowel sounds occur in more two- to three-letter words, whereas long vowels create more four- or more letter words: *mate, fate*). Be mindful of letters that can cause some sound confusion, such as *b* and *v*, or *f* and *v*; or letters that can be confused physically, such as *b* and *d*, and *p* and *q*.

Teachers may wonder how quickly to introduce new letters. Research recommends a letter-a-day approach rather than a letter-a-week approach, with each lesson lasting no more than 15 minutes (Reutzel 2015). Progress from naming the letter, offering the sound of the letter, and distinguishing uppercase from lowercase, to finding the letter in text or in the classroom, and finally, to writing the letter. Begin the 15 minutes with an explicit introduction to the letter of the day, "This is the letter *Tt*," showing both the uppercase and lowercase letters and asking children to repeat the name of the letter. Next, share the sound the letter represents and ask children to repeat the sound. Provide tangible forms of the upper- and lowercase letter, such as cardboard cutouts or magnets, and have children sort them. Then provide a page of text and ask children to find examples of the upper- and lowercase *t*. Finally, have children write both upper- and lowercase *t*. By introducing a letter a day, teachers can revisit the letters throughout the year and begin to make words more quickly than in the 26 weeks (more than six months!) required if introducing a letter a week.

The goal of instruction at the partial alphabetic phase is for readers to develop automaticity with sounds and letters, preparing them for aspects of word recognition where their cognitive focus will shift to meaning making (Scarborough 2001). Word recognition includes instruction in *phonics* (the study of speech sounds related to reading), *decoding* (using the understanding of letter-sound relationships to decipher a word), *encoding* (using decoding knowledge to produce letter patterns when spelling), *sight words* (words recognized immediately, often consisting of high-frequency words), and *fluency* (reading with accuracy, pacing, and expression).

The Full Alphabetic and the Consolidated Alphabetic Phases: Phonics, Spelling, Sight Words, and Fluency

Sight-word recognition and automaticity develop during the full alphabetic phase and the consolidated alphabetic phase. In this stage the focus is on *phonics* (the relationship between sounds and their spellings). Phonics instruction is the teaching of letter-sound (grapheme-phoneme) relationships. As previously discussed, there are three dominant approaches to phonics instruction: 1) synthetic, 2) analytic, and 3) analogy-based (Ehri 2014). Regardless of the approach, the research is clear that children benefit from *systematic* (following a scope and sequence) and *explicit* (direct teaching) instruction in phonics (Ehri et al. 2001; NRP 2000; Shanahan 2018b; Snow and Juel 2005; Wanzek et al. 2018).

> Systematic instruction in phonics is essential for students to become fluent readers (Ehri 2020). This means explicitly teaching young readers how to match the letter of the alphabet to the one or more sounds (*phonemes*) it represents.

Systematic instruction in phonics is essential for students to become fluent readers (Ehri 2020). This means explicitly teaching young readers how to match the letter of the alphabet to the one or more sounds (*phonemes*) it represents. For example, the letter *g* can make two sounds: a hard sound like the *g* in *dig*, or a soft sound like the *g* in *gem*. Introduce high-utility sounds and spellings first (e.g., /ă/, *a*; /m/, *m*; /t/, *t*) so that students can begin to blend through words and move through the phases. Practice words in context so students can cement the syntactic and semantic correspondence of those words (Ehri 2020). This consistent practice builds a sight-word bank that readers can use when encountering text.

Decoding and Encoding: The Reading and Spelling Connection

Decoding and encoding have a reciprocal relationship. While decoding is taking the sounds off the page to read words, encoding (spelling) is the production of letters to represent sounds. Allowing children in the pre-alphabetic and the partial alphabetic stages to write using invented spelling can be a valuable literacy strategy (Adams 2011). For instance, encouraging young readers to sound out words as they spell them reinforces matching letters to sounds (e.g., /k/ /ă/ /t/ *cat*). This in turn builds their phonics knowledge. The same grapheme-phoneme relationships readers rely on for word recognition in reading are called upon for spelling. Spelling patterns can also be referred to as *orthography*. A student's ability to accurately map letters and letter combinations to sounds and store these in memory (*orthographic mapping*) is crucial to spelling development. Knowledge of words and word parts is essential to reading and spelling, and readers must be able to apply this knowledge accurately and efficiently. This process of studying words and word parts is known as *word study*. An integrated approach to word study includes instruction in spelling, phonics, and vocabulary.

> Knowledge of words and word parts is essential to reading and spelling, and readers must be able to apply this knowledge accurately and efficiently.

Beginning readers will encounter unknown words when encoding (trying to spell a word), either mentally (when looking for a word) or physically (when writing). It is inefficient, and probably impossible, to memorize the spelling of thousands of words, so it makes sense to be strategic. Effective spelling instruction is explicit about, and takes advantage of, the relationships between how words look, how they sound, and what they mean, integrating and enhancing readers' existing decoding knowledge and building strategies for word analysis.

What do we do when we encounter unknown words? How do we apply our knowledge? As readers advance to the consolidated alphabetic phase, they will strategically apply knowledge of morphemes (the smallest grammatical unit that carries meaning, such as *re–*, *–ing*, *–ed*) to decode unfamiliar multisyllabic words (Ehri 2014). "Through this process, as the connections between spelling, sound, and meaning become completely and reliably represented and bound together, the word will become readable at a glance, it will become a 'sight word'" (Adams 2011, 17).

Sight-Word Automaticity

For readers to advance through the phases, it is crucial that they build a sight-word bank. Sight words are words readers know automatically, without having to sound them out (sometimes referred to as *automaticity*). Research shows that recognition of symbols, signs, and other tokens is a form of visual learning that can support sight-word automaticity. "Visual learning is a style of learning that utilizes visual input (symbols, icons, pictures, illustrations) to obtain new information. . . . Educators, parents, and caregivers can utilize visual cues to help expand a toddler's vocabulary and boost language development" (BabySparks 2020). Children in prekindergarten might recognize only their own names. "Most state standards specify that children need to know some letter names and sounds, and be able to recognize sounds at the beginning and end of words and words that rhyme, before entering kindergarten" (Burchinal et al. 2022, 46). Continued, repeated exposure to words through explicit instruction and word play is a must to build automaticity. Plan word-study instruction in ways that foster automaticity and continue to build reading skills in and out of context.

Fluency

Over time, a large sight-word bank coupled with strategic decoding skills can lead students to become fluent readers. *Fluency* is the ability to read fluidly. Fluent reading has three aspects—accuracy, pacing, and expression. When fluent readers read aloud, their reading is accurate, at a quick but natural pace, and has expression. When fluent readers read silently, reading is highly automatic, with readers grouping words together for meaning rather than reading word by word. When readers attain an appropriate level of fluency, they can dedicate their attention to comprehension. Instruction that builds decoding skills and automaticity supports fluency. Additional explicit instruction and practice in pace, proper expression, vocabulary, and language structures aid the development of fluent readers. For young learners, awareness of fluency develops as they have opportunities to observe and listen to adults read and model fluent reading across genre and text type. For example, when adults read with character voices, children hear expressiveness, a quality of fluent reading. Modeling fluent reading every day, having books available for children to read on their own, inviting opportunities to demonstrate expression, and repeated and assisted reading are all strategies shown to support fluency (Rasinski et al. 2017).

The Importance of a Print-Rich Environment

There are four dimensions to print-rich classroom environments: providing literacy tools or props, effective placement of these tools, using the tools during literacy instruction, and promoting use of these tools in the classroom (Wolfersberger et al. 2004, 216). The first dimension, *literacy tools*, refers to items such as paper, pencils, books and magazines, adult-

and child-authored materials, computers, and so on. The four dimensions are intentional and interconnected. Purposeful selection of relevant tools, and continued interaction with and modeling of their use, engages children in multiple aspects of literacy development.

Effective ways to create a print-rich environment include providing a variety of reading and writing materials and multiple ways students can interact with them, either individually or in groups. Some materials should be available all the time, and others may be brought out based on topics being studied. Books, computers, word walls, and dictionaries encourage children to seek out resources for assistance. Labels and pictures connect words and symbols to meaning and understanding. Teachers introduce vocabulary through speaking and written text, and encourage students to use oral and written language in return. Show children how literacy is used in daily activities by displaying maps, recipes, menus, or signs around the room. Foster writing by providing diverse materials, including markers, crayons, chalk, magnetic writing boards, keyboards, or paints, for children to use to express their ideas. Set up the room so that children encounter these materials naturally and can integrate their use with ease.

> Effective ways to create a print-rich environment include providing a variety of reading and writing materials and multiple ways students can interact with them, either individually or in groups.

Model literacy-rich activities such as discussing an upcoming walk or field trip and examining a map or reading and displaying the directions for a game. This shows students the functional value of written and spoken words. Finally, be sure that the environment is representative of the diversity of our world today. Consider children's backgrounds and learning frameworks, and honor these in the images and words available in the classroom environment.

Putting It All Together

Teachers of emergent and early readers have a huge responsibility, assisting students in moving through the phases of word reading. The development of phonemic awareness and strong orthographic representations paves the way for quick, accurate decoding and encoding, freeing up cognitive resources for comprehension and expression. Providing explicit instruction and print-rich environments and frequently reading aloud are essential to developing children's foundational literacy skills.

What Is a Word?

Objective

- Separate (segment) sentences into individual words.

Background Information

Phonological and phonemic awareness develop step by step. Students move from hearing individual words in sentences to identifying each word in a compound word to counting syllables in words. Experts recommend first having students practice isolating words in a sentence to develop their understanding of what a word is (Foorman et al. 2016). Identifying the unique words in sentences supports students' ability to hear smaller and smaller sound segments (syllables, onsets and rimes, and phonemes).

Materials

- counters (*optional*)

Process

1. Place students side by side in a line with plenty of space for them to move forward.
2. Say a simple sentence aloud. For example, "I like toys."
3. Have students repeat the sentence several times.
4. Model how to take one step forward as you say each word in the sentence. Then have students take a step forward for each word in the sentence.
5. Continue with additional sentences. Use other actions once students get the idea of making a forward movement for matching a word, for example, hops, jumps, and skips.

Differentiation

During the Lesson: Provide an initial model with each new sentence for as long as students need it, but build toward independence. Hold the hands of students who need additional support and move with them. Work toward longer and longer sentences that require students to hold more words in their heads. Reinforce the concept during small-group time by providing students with counters or squares of construction paper. Have students move one counter for each word in a sentence. Encourage students to come up with their own sentences to use with the activity.

After the Lesson: Once students understand to take a step for each word, this is a great transition activity to move students from one area of the classroom to another. For example, when students are sitting on the carpet and it is time to go back to their desks, have them stand up and face their desks. Provide a sentence. Have students take one step for each word in the sentence as they walk toward their desks. Once students have reached their desks, have them sit down, even if they are not done saying the sentence.

Working with Words— Compound Words

Objectives

- Blend individual words into compound words.
- Segment compound words into individual words.

Background Information

Phonological and phonemic awareness develop step by step. Students move from hearing individual words in sentences to identifying each word in a compound word to counting syllables in words. Blending or segmenting the two words of a compound provides the scaffold of allowing students to hear whole words as individual parts. Working with compound words helps students understand that some words can be broken into smaller words. Identifying the unique words in compounds is recommended (Foorman et al. 2016) and helps students learn to hear smaller and smaller sound segments (syllables, onsets and rime, and phonemes).

Materials

- *Compound Word Picture Cards* (page 35)

Process

1. Tell students they will be putting two words together to make a new word.
2. Hold up, but keep apart, two picture cards that together create a compound word— for example, *basket* and *ball* (*basketball*). Say the name of each word and have students repeat them.
3. Put the word cards right next to each other and have students combine the two words together to create the compound word (*basketball*).
4. Continue creating other compound words. See the list on page 33 for all the compound words that can be made with the *Compound Word Picture Cards*.
5. When students are skilled at making compound words with visual support, complete the same activity without visual support. See page 34 for additional compound words.

Differentiation

During the Lesson: Model saying the two words and the compound word for students who have difficulty combining them. Have them repeat what you say. Then say and display the two words and have the student combine the words together to name the compound word independently.

After the Lesson: When students can easily combine two words, have them take away one of the words of the compound word. For example, tell students, "Say *basketball* without *basket*." Provide visual support for students by displaying the two picture cards for the compound word and then taking away one card, leaving only the picture card for the word students should say. Work toward independence without the visual support. See the *Compound Words List* (page 34) for additional words.

Compound Word Pictures

basket + ball = basketball

butter + fly = butterfly

cup + cake = cupcake

eye + ball = eyeball

fire + fly = firefly

mail + box = mailbox

pan + cake = pancake

rain + bow = rainbow

rain + coat = raincoat

sand + box = sandbox

skate + board = skateboard

snow + ball = snowball

snow + board = snowboard

Compound Words

afternoon	airplane	armpit	babysitter
backbone	background	ballpark	baseball
bathroom	bedtime	birthday	blackbird
blackout	bookshelf	bookworm	bulldog
buttercup	butterfly	candlelight	catfish
classmate	daydream	dishwasher	doorbell
dragonfly	earring	earthworm	eggshell
eyeglasses	eyelash	eyelid	fingernail
fingerprint	firefly	firehouse	fireworks
flashlight	footprint	forehead	friendship
goldfish	goodbye	goodnight	grapefruit
grasshopper	haircut	hamburger	headache
heartbeat	highway	hilltop	homework
honeybee	jackpot	jellybean	jellyfish
ladybug	lifeguard	lighthouse	lipstick
matchbox	milkshake	motorcycle	myself
nearby	newspaper	notebook	outdoors
password	ponytail	popcorn	postcard
rainfall	roadrunner	sailboat	scarecrow
seafood	seashore	skateboard	starlight
strawberry	sunglasses	sunrise	sunroof
sunset	sunshine	teacup	teaspoon
today	toolbox	underwear	upstairs
wallpaper	watermelon	weekend	wheelchair

Compound Word Picture Cards

Compound Word Picture Cards

Compound Word Picture Cards

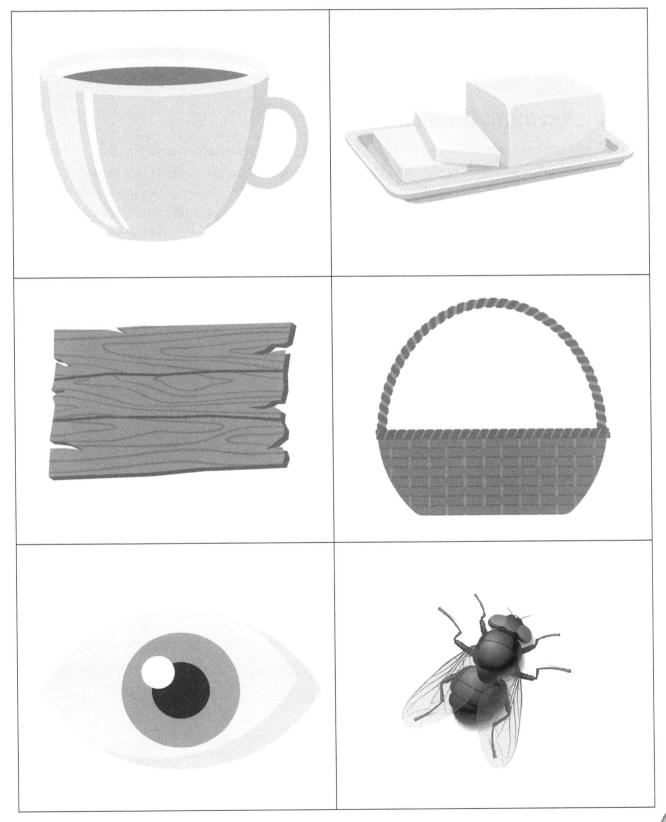

Silly Willy Rhyming Words

Objectives

- Demonstrate understanding of spoken words and sound parts in words.
- Recognize rhyming words.

Background Information

To recognize rhymes, children must notice similarities in how words sound. Rhyme recognition is one aspect of phonological awareness and requires that students attend to larger parts of words, specifically the *rime* (the part of a syllable that includes the vowel and any consonants that follow). In this activity, students are given a silly word that rhymes with the name for a real object that is in front of them, providing the visual support for identifying the rhyming word.

Materials

- classroom objects such as a crayon, book, pen, cup, box, and so on
- puppet or stuffed animal

Process

1. Set out the objects where students can see them. Review the name of each object to ensure students know how it will be identified.

2. Introduce your puppet, Silly Willy. Tell students that *Silly* and *Willy* rhyme because they both have *-illy* in them. Have students repeat the following: "*Silly, Willy*, they both have *-illy*."

3. Tell students that Silly Willy always says a word that rhymes with another word.

4. Choose one of the objects, but rather than say its name, have Silly Willy say a made-up rhyming word. For example, if the word you want students to guess is *book*, have Silly Willy say *zook*.

5. Ask students to name the object Silly Willy's word rhymes with. Students should identify *book* as the rhyming word. Then have students say, "*Zook, book*, they both have *-ook*."

6. Continue with other objects.

Differentiation

During the Lesson: Limit the number of objects displayed to begin with. As students show an understanding for the task, increase the number of objects to increase the number of words they must choose from.

After the Lesson: Allow students to play the role of Silly Willy and be the ones to name silly rhymes for real objects.

Create New Nursery Rhymes

Objectives

- Demonstrate understanding of spoken words and sound parts in words.
- Recognize and produce rhyming words.

Background Information

Words that rhyme are words that end with the same stressed vowel and final consonant sound(s). Generating rhymes demonstrates an ability to manipulate initial sounds in words, while keeping the final sounds the same. Creating words that rhyme is often difficult for young children. In this activity, students play with the rhyming words in a nursery rhyme to create new rhymes. This requires that children listen closely for sounds within words and helps build their awareness that words are made up of separate parts.

Materials

- a nursery rhyme
- yarn (*optional*)

Process

1. Select a nursery rhyme such as "Higglety Pigglety Pop," and write it on chart paper. Practice the nursery rhyme over the course of several days until students can say it by memory. As students are learning the rhyme, use it to teach different concepts such as one-to-one word correspondence, left-to-right tracking, return sweep, and punctuation.

   Higglety Pigglety Pop
   Higglety, pigglety, pop,
   The dog has eaten the mop;
   The pig's in a hurry,
   The cat's in a flurry,
   Higglety, pigglety, pop.

2. Help students create a new version of the nursery rhyme by replacing the rhyming words. To do this, replace the rime in rhyming words with a different rime. For example, in "Higglety Pigglety Pop," replace words with *-op* with words with *-ap*. Practice saying the new nursery rhyme.

Higglety Pigglety Pap
Higglety, pigglety, *pap*,
The dog has eaten the *map*;
The pig's in a hurry,
The cat's in a flurry,
Higglety, pigglety, *pap*.

Differentiation

During the Lesson: Write the rhyming words where students can see them, and have students compare the letters that are the same and different. Help students realize words that rhyme have the same middle and ending letters.

After the Lesson: Display the nursery rhyme chart with a pointer, and allow students to practice reading it on their own. Tie several lengths of yarn into circles, and have students place them around the words that rhyme.

Suggested Nursery Rhymes

Jack and Jill

Humpty Dumpty

Twinkle, Twinkle Little Star

Little Jack Horner

Baa, Baa Black Sheep

Feel the Syllables

Objectives

- Demonstrate understanding of spoken words and syllables.
- Identify and segment syllables in spoken words.

Background Information

Syllables are uninterrupted sound units organized around vowel sounds. Every syllable has a vowel sound, and that vowel sound may or may not have a consonant sound before or after it. Syllables are sometimes referred to as the "beats" or "pulses" in a word (Yopp and Yopp 2022). With this strategy, children quite literally feel those beats in words. Together students will count the syllables in the names of their classmates. Then, students will apply their knowledge of syllables by sorting words into categories of one, two, or three or more syllables. Students will first sort names and can sort other categories of words in future lessons.

Materials

- photos of students
- chart paper

Process

1. Tell students that words have parts called *syllables* and that some words have one syllable and others have more.

2. Explain that we can feel syllables by how our mouth moves as we say words. Model how to place the back of your hand flat and just under your chin.

3. Tell students to watch your chin drop and hit your hand as you say a word. Start with a closed mouth. Say the word *recess*.

4. Explain to students that your chin bumped your hand for each syllable, so for the word *recess*, your chin bumped your hand two times. Have students place their hands under their chins and say the word *recess*.

5. Use students' names to have students practice feeling their chins bump their hands for the syllables. Say a student's name. Have students repeat it. Then have students place their hands under their chins to feel the syllables. Continue with other students' names.

6. Chart words by the number of syllables. Create a three-column chart and label the top of each column: *1 syllable*, *2 syllables*, and *3+ syllables*. Work with the class to sort the students' photos into the correct columns (by number of syllables in their names). Make the chart and photos available for students to repeat the activity independently or with partners.

7. Repeat the process on subsequent days using different categories, such as color words, animals, sports, or school supplies. Provide pictures that correspond with the words.

Differentiation

During the Lesson: Provide additional support for students as needed by tapping or clapping the syllables while students place their hands under their chins. The sound of a tap or clap helps some students notice the beat as they feel their chins drop.

After the Lesson: Use the strategy with content vocabulary words. For example, you could use it when introducing the word *forecast* during a science unit about weather.

Making Sandwiches with Onsets and Rimes

Objectives

- Demonstrate understanding of spoken words and sounds in words.
- Blend and segment onsets and rimes of single-syllable spoken words.

Background Information

Blending onsets and rimes into words and segmenting words into onsets and rimes is an important part of phonological awareness for young literacy learners. Onsets and rimes are parts of syllables. The *onset* in a syllable is the segment preceding the vowel. For example, the onset of *bat* is /b/. The *rime* in a syllable is the vowel and the sounds that follow. In the word *bat*, the rime is /ăt/. As children learn to play with words, language becomes exciting for learners. To enhance phonological awareness, complete this activity orally, without the use of any print (Jump and Johnson 2023).

Materials

- *Rime Word List* (page 45)
- *Onset Word List* (page 47)

Process

1. Segment a word into its onset and rime. Hold out your right palm as you say the onset. Hold out your left hand as you say the rime. For example, if the word is *cat*, say /k/ as you hold out your right palm. Say /ăt/ as you hold out your left palm. Have students repeat both the onset and rime as they hold out their palms. (Students can "mirror" your hand motions.)

2. Show students how to "make sandwiches" by clapping their hands together as they blend the onset and rime to say the whole word, *cat*.

3. Continue, using words with the same rime, for example: *fat, sat, mat, pat,* and *bat*. (See the *Rime Word List* on page 45.) After you segment the word, have students "make a sandwich" to blend the onset and rime.

4. Once students are skilled at blending words that rhyme, use words with the same onset and different rimes, for example: *cab, can, cat, car,* and *cap*. (See the *Onset Word List* on page 47.)

Differentiation

During the Lesson: If students are having difficulty blending the onset and rime, model how to blend them and have students repeat the word. This tells students what they are listening for and provides multiple chances for them to work with the same word before going on to the next word.

After the Lesson: When students are skilled at blending onset and rime, reverse the process. Provide students a word and have students segment the onset and rime.

Rime Word List

a	cab	bad	bam	cap	bat
	dab	dad	dam	gap	cat
	fab	fad	gam	lap	fat
	gab	had	ham	map	hat
	jab	lad	Pam	nap	mat
	lab	mad	ram	rap	pat
	nab	pad	Sam	sap	rat
	tab	rad	yam	tap	sat
		sad		zap	vat
e	bed	beg	gem	Ben	bet
	fed	keg	hem	den	get
	led	leg		hen	jet
	red	Meg		Jen	let
	Ted	peg		men	met
	wed			pen	net
				ten	pet
				yen	set
					vet
					wet

(continued)

Rime Word List (continued)

i	bid	big	bin	dip	bit
	did	dig	din	hip	fit
	hid	fig	kin	lip	hit
	kid	gig	pin	nip	kit
	lid	jig	tin	pip	lit
	mid	pig	win	rip	pit
	rid	rig		sip	sit
		wig		tip	wit
		zig		zip	
o	cod	bog	con	bop	cot
	mod	cog	Jon	cop	dot
	nod	dog	Ron	hop	got
	pod	fog	son	lop	hot
	rod	hog	ton	mop	lot
	sod	jog	won	pop	not
		log		sop	pot
				top	rot
u	cub	bug	bum	bun	but
	hub	dug	gum	fun	cut
	pub	hug	hum	gun	gut
	rub	jug	sum	nun	hut
	sub	mug	yum	pun	jut
	tub	rug		run	nut
		tug		sun	rut

Onset Word List

b	d	f	g	h	j	l	m	p	r	s	t
bad	dab	fab	gab	had	jab	lab	mad	pad	rad	sad	tab
bag	dad	fad	gag	ham	jag	lad	man	pal	rag	sag	tad
bam	Dan	fan	gap	has	jam	lag	map	Pam	ram	Sam	tag
ban		far	gas	hat	Jan	lap	mat	pan	rap	sap	tan
bar		fat			jar			par	rat	sat	tap
bat					jaw			pat			tar
bay					jay						tat
											tax
bed	Deb	fed	gel	hem	Jed	led	med	ped	red	set	Ted
beg	den		gem	hen	Jen	leg	Meg	Peg	ref		ten
Ben			gen	her	jet	let	Mel	pen	rep		Tex
bet			get	hey			met	pep	Rex		
Bev								pet			
bib	dib	fib	gig	hid	jib	lid	mid	pig	rib	sip	Tim
bid	did	fig		him	Jim	lip	mix	pin	rid	sis	tin
big	dig	fin		hip		lit		pip	rig	sit	tip
bin	dim	fit		his				pit	rim	six	
bit	dip	fix		hit					rip		
bob	doc	fob	gob	hob	job	lob	mob	pod	rob	sob	Tom
bog	dog	fog	got	hog	jog	log	mod	pop	rod	sod	ton
bop	dot	for		hop	jot	lop	mom	pot	Ron	sog	top
bot				hot		lot	mop	pox	rot	son	tot
box										sop	
boy											
bub	dub	fun	gum	hub	jug	lug	mud	pub	rub	sub	tub
bud	dud	fur	gun	hug	jut		mug	pug	rug	sum	tug
bug	dug		Gus	hum			mum	pun	run	sun	tut
bun			gut	hut				pup	rut	sup	tux
bus								put			
but											
buy											

Isolating Sounds with Movement

Objectives

- Demonstrate understanding of sounds (phonemes).
- Isolate phonemes of spoken single-syllable words.

Background Information

Segmenting words into individual phonemes (or sounds) is an important aspect of phonological awareness. Phonological awareness is essential for reading because of the relationship between the spoken word and the written word. The ability to recognize and manipulate sounds in spoken language is required to learn letter-sound correspondence (Ehri et al. 2001; Kilpatrick 2015, 2016; Moats 2020b; Yopp and Yopp 2022). With this strategy, students will physically use their bodies to segment individual sounds (phonemes) in a spoken word. The goal is to strengthen students' ability to isolate initial, medial vowel, and final sounds when given a whole word by the teacher.

Materials

- list of consonant-vowel-consonant (CVC) words

Process

1. Have students stand far enough apart so they will not touch other students as they move their arms around.

2. Use arm movements to help students isolate sounds in various positions in words. Students will move their extended arms in an arch from one side of their bodies, over their heads, to the other side of their bodies. Each position represents a sound in a CVC word.

3. Say a word such as *cat* and ask students to repeat it. Then have students stretch out their arms and use the following motions as the class segments the sounds in the word—/k/ /ă/ /t/. If you are facing students, remember to mirror them as you provide examples

   - Students' arms extended out to the left represents the initial sound in a word.
   - Students' arms extended over their heads represents the medial sound in a word.
   - Students' arms extended out to the right represents the final sound in a word.

4. Have students follow the directions on page 49 to isolate specific sounds in words.

Initial Sound	Medial Sound	Final sound
Students punch their fists out to the left as they extend their arms when they say the initial sound in the word.	Students stretch the medial sound in the word as they move their arms over their heads.	Students punch their fists out to the right as they extend their arms when they say the final sound in the word.

Differentiation

During the Lesson: Start with having students isolate initial sounds and punch their fists to the left (*cat*, /k/). Move to final sounds after students have practiced initial sounds (*cat*, /t/). Medial sounds are usually the most difficult for students to hear. Move to medial sounds once students are secure with initial and final sounds.

After the Lesson: Place picture cards of CVC words in a center. Have students work with partners to practice saying the words while using the arm positions.

Sound Boxes

Objectives

- Demonstrate understanding of spoken words and sounds (phonemes).
- Segment phonemes of single-syllable spoken words.

Background Information

Phonemic awareness practice provides children with opportunities to manipulate language. The goal of Sound Boxes is to strengthen emergent readers' ability to isolate initial, medial vowel, and final sounds when given a whole word by the teacher (Keesey, Konrad, and Joseph 2015). Oral language manipulation is essential for emergent readers to become aware that whole words consist of individual sounds. Begin by using words with two phonemes and increase the difficulty by progressing to words with three and four phonemes.

Materials

- *Sound Boxes: Three Sounds* (page 52)
- *Sound Boxes: Four Sounds* (page 53)
- counters (3–4 per student)

Process

1. Prior to this lesson, prepare Sound Boxes mats. Make copies of *Sound Boxes: Three Sounds* on cardstock and place them in sheet protectors. This protects the mats as they are reused.

2. Choose a word family that will be practiced using the mat. See the Onset Word List (page 47) or Rime Word List (page 45) for ideas.

3. Have students place counters in the top row of boxes.

4. Say a word. Model how to segment the word into its phonemes as you move the counters from the top row into the second row of boxes, one for each sound. For example: *hat*. Move the first counter as you say /h/, the second counter as you say /ă/, and the third counter as you say /t/.

5. Blend the sounds to say the word and run your finger along the arrow.

6. Have students repeat the process on their mats.

7. Repeat several words in one word family before moving on to another word family.

8. When students are ready, stop modeling how to segment words. Say a word and let students segment it on their own.

Differentiation

During the Lesson: Challenge students with longer words by using *Sound Boxes: Four Sounds*. Have students place counters in all four boxes in the top row. Say a word with three or four sounds. Have students determine how many sounds they hear in the word and move the appropriate number of counters as they say the sounds. Repeat with additional words of three or four sounds.

After the Lesson: Once students become skilled at segmenting the sounds in a word, have students record the letter that represents each sound on the mat and read the word. After students have segmented the word and moved the counters from the top row of boxes to the bottom row of boxes, ask students to move the first counter from the bottom row back to the top row as they say the sound again and use erasable markers to write the letter that represents that sound. They continue moving the counters from the bottom row to the top row and recording the letters.

Sound Boxes: Three Sounds

Directions: Listen to your teacher. Say the sounds. Push the counters into the boxes.

Literacy Strategies—131696

© Shell Education

Sound Boxes: Four Sounds

Directions: Listen to your teacher. Say the sounds. Push the counters into the boxes.

Introducing Letters and Sounds

Objectives

- Recognize and name uppercase and lowercase letters.
- Produce the primary sound for each letter of the alphabet.

Background Information

The *alphabetic principle* is the understanding that sounds are represented by letters, and letters represent sounds. Understanding the alphabetic principle and making letter-sound connections prepares students for instruction in word recognition. Explicit instruction in letters and sounds is necessary for many students. Students' understanding of the alphabetic principle does not occur in one lesson, but rather develops over time as students have many opportunities to practice and apply their understanding of the relationships between sounds and letters.

Materials

- letter cards
- key word pictures
- hand mirrors (*optional*)

Process

Use the steps below to introduce individual letters. See Guiding Principles for Introducing Letters (page 55) for considerations regarding the order of letter introduction.

1. **Say the sound**.
   Make the sound represented by the letter e.g., /s/. Then, introduce a key word that begins with the sound. Choose a key word that, when spoken, enables the sound to be clearly heard. For example, *sun*.

2. **Describe the mouth movements**, or *articulatory gestures* (the actions needed to make the sound).
   Describe what is happening with the lips, tongue, and throat as the sound is produced. For example, for /f/, the mouth is almost completely closed and the top teeth rest lightly on the bottom lip. The tongue is in the middle of the mouth, not touching teeth. There is a small airflow that can be continued while making the sound.

3. **Use a key picture and physical gesture**.
   Display a picture of the key word. See *Alphabet Sound Chart* (page 58) for an example. Create a gesture the students will use to remember the sound. For example, for /ĭ/, students can itch their noses as they make the sound. It can be helpful if the gesture relates to the key word.

4. **Describe the shape of the letter**.
   Display or write the letter, both uppercase and lowercase, and name them as the letters that represent the sound. Describe how the letter looks. Does it have straight lines or curves, or both? Is it a tall letter or short letter? Do the uppercase and lowercase letters look the same or different? Is there more than one way to write the letter, e.g., does the letter look different depending on the font used?

5. **Describe how to form the letter**.
   Use verbal pathways to describe and model how to form the letter. For example, for the letter *T*, pull down, then go across at the top line.

> ## Guiding Principles for Introducing Letters
>
> - Provide explicit and systematic instruction.
>
> - Introduce letters that have high utility first.
>
> - Begin with consonants that have continuous sounds.
>
> - Separate the introduction of letters that are visually similar such as *b*, *d*, *p*, and *q*.
>
> - Separate the introduction of letters that are auditorily similar, such as *f* /f/ and *v* /v/.

Differentiation

During the Lesson: Have students pay close attention to your mouth as you say the sound represented by the letter. Provide small hand mirrors for students to use as they focus on their mouth positions, especially for letters that sound similar to others, such as *m* /m/ and *n* /n/.

After the Lesson: Have students use multisensory writing to practice forming the letters introduced. See Multisensory Letter Formation Practice (page 141).

Alphabet Sound Chart

Objectives

- Recognize and name uppercase and lowercase letters.
- Produce the primary sound for each letter of the alphabet.

Background Information

Explicit phonics instruction is necessary for students to easily and quickly recognize letter-sound relationships (NRP 2000). This knowledge will help students become efficient, automatic decoders of written text. Students' understanding of the alphabetic principle does not occur in one lesson, but rather develops over time as students have many opportunities to practice and apply their understanding of the relationships between sounds and letters.

Materials

- *Alphabet Sound Chart* (page 58)
- plastic letters or small letter cards
- counters or small toys

Process

Make copies of the *Alphabet Sound Chart*. Laminate them or place them in sheet protectors. Use the chart for the following activities.

- **Alphabet Song:** Have students sing the *ABC* song as they point to each letter on the chart.
- **Alphabet Sound Chant:** Have students point to each letter as they say the name of the letter, then the name of the sound and the key word. For example, "A, a, /ă/, apple." Continue for each letter.
- **Hand Gesture:** Develop a hand gesture that corresponds with each key word. Have students make the gesture as they say the letter, sound, or word.
- **Letter/Sound/Word Find:** Provide each student with a counter or small toy. Name a letter, sound, or key word from the *Alphabet Sound Chart*. Have students locate the correct letter or sound and place their counter on that box. Work toward rapid automaticity.

- **Letter Match-Up:** Provide students with plastic letters or small letter cards and have them match each letter to the corresponding box on the *Alphabet Sound Chart*. Work toward rapid automaticity.

- **Alphabetical Order:** Cut out the squares on the *Alphabet Sound Chart* and have students put the letters in order.

Differentiation

During the Lesson: Have students slow down when singing *l, m, n, o,* and *p* to ensure one-to-one correspondence. Once students can sing the alphabet, have them say the alphabet as they point to the *Alphabet Sound Chart* rather than sing it.

After the Lesson: Name a word that is not shown on the *Alphabet Sound Chart* and have students determine the sound of the beginning letter and put a marker on the corresponding box.

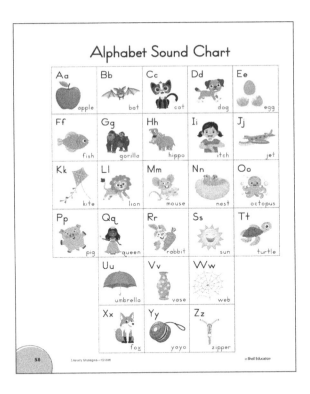

Alphabet Sound Chart

Aa apple	**Bb** bat	**Cc** cat	**Dd** dog	**Ee** egg
Ff fish	**Gg** gorilla	**Hh** hippo	**Ii** itch	**Jj** jet
Kk kite	**Ll** lion	**Mm** mouse	**Nn** nest	**Oo** octopus
Pp pig	**Qq** queen	**Rr** rabbit	**Ss** sun	**Tt** turtle
Uu umbrella	**Vv** vase	**Ww** web		
Xx fox	**Yy** yoyo	**Zz** zipper		

Working with an Alphabet Arc

Objectives

- Recognize and name uppercase and lowercase letters.
- Produce the primary sound for each letter of the alphabet.

Background Information

Explicit phonics instruction is necessary for students to easily and quickly recognize letter-sound relationships (NRP 2000). This knowledge will help students become efficient, automatic decoders of written text. Students' understanding of the alphabetic principle does not occur in one lesson, but rather develops over time, thus necessitating the need for many opportunities for students to practice. Working with an Alphabet Arc provides students the opportunity to interact with both uppercase and lowercase letters and enables the teacher to scaffold instruction to meet students' varying needs.

Materials

- *Uppercase Alphabet Arc* (pages 61–62)
- *Lowercase Alphabet Arc* (pages 63–64)
- *Uppercase Letters* (page 65)
- *Lowercase Letters* (page 66)
- *Alphabet Sound Chart* (page 58)

Process

Prepare an Alphabet Arc mat for each child. Make copies of the two *Uppercase Alphabet Arc* pages. Copy the *Lowercase Alphabet Arc* pages onto the back of the *Uppercase Alphabet Arc* pages. Tape the two pages together to make an arc with the uppercase letters on one side and the lowercase letters on the back. Laminate the arcs for durability and for use with erasable markers. Make copies of *Uppercase Letters* and *Lowercase Letters*. Cut them apart and laminate them. Use the arc mats and letters for the following progression of activities.

- Provide students with the alphabet arc with the lowercase side facing up. Have students sing the alphabet song while pointing to each letter. The intent here is not yet for letter recognition, but for one-to-one correspondence. Practice every day until students have one-to-one correspondence. When students demonstrate good one-to-one correspondence, move on to the next activity.

- Provide students with the lowercase letters. Have students place each letter above the corresponding lowercase letter on the alphabet arc. This creates a second, larger arc outside the mat arc. Have students name the letters. If students do not know the name of a letter, have them find the letter that matches on the alphabet arc and then sing the alphabet song while pointing to each letter on the alphabet arc to find the name of the letter. Begin with the most common letters and letters in children's names, and limit the number of letters students work with initially. Continue to add letters in subsequent days and weeks.

- Have students name the sounds the letters represent. If students do not know a sound, provide them with an *Alphabet Sound Chart* and have them find the corresponding letter and use the key picture to help identify the sound.

Build to rapid automaticity in completing the activities described above. Then begin working on some of the following extensions.

- **Letter Writing:** Name a letter and ask students to move the letter card from outside the arc to the empty space inside the arc. Have students use the letter card as a model and write the letter on the mat using an erasable marker.

- **Uppercase/Lowercase Match:** Alternate which alphabet arc and letters students work with. For example, have students use the *Uppercase Alphabet Arc* and lowercase letters. Work toward automaticity with letter matching.

- **Making Words:** After the letter cards are placed around the arc, say a CVC word. Have students segment the word, take the letter cards from outside the arc, and place them inside the arc to build the word.

Differentiation

During the Lesson: Place your hand over a student's hand to assist them in gaining one-to-one correspondence while singing the alphabet. Sing the alphabet song with students. Slow down when singing the letters *l, m, n, o,* and *p.*

After the Lesson: Say CVC words and have students write the words in the center of the arc without moving letter cards. Students can refer to the arc to see what each letter looks like.

N O P Q R S T U V W X Y Z

a b c d e f g h i j k l m

n o p q r s t u v w x y z

Uppercase Letters

A	B	C	D	E
F	G	H	I	J
K	L	M	N	O
P	Q	R	S	T
	U	V	W	
	X	Y	Z	

Lowercase Letters

a b c d e

f g h i j

k l m n o

p q r s t

u v w

x y z

Literacy Strategies—131696   © Shell Education

Alphabet Sorts

Objective

- Recognize and name uppercase and lowercase letters.

Background Information

Foundational to the alphabetic principle and reading is the ability to recognize letters. Alphabet Sorts are essentially categorizing letters by similarity. The process of categorization requires readers to look closely at letters to identify the shapes of lines (straight or curved), height of lines, and other letter features. In doing so, students build and reinforce their understandings that help them make sense of and recognize letters.

Materials

- *Large Uppercase Letter Cards* (page 68)
- *Large Lowercase Letter Cards* (page 73)
- index cards

Process

1. Choose a set of letters students will work with. Decide on the features by which students will sort the letters. Write the names of the features on index cards. Suggested features include:

   - Uppercase/Lowercase

   - Matching uppercase letters to lowercase letters

   - Tall letters (letters that touch the top line of lined writing paper); short letters (letters that touch the middle line of lined writing paper); low letters (letters that fall below the bottom line of lined writing paper)

   - Letters with only straight lines, letters with only curved lines, and letters with both straight and curved lines

2. Have students sort the letters by feature.

Differentiation

During the Lesson: Have students describe the features of letters. For example, the letter *F* has a tall line and two short lines. Add rigor to the activity by mixing uppercase and lowercase letters in the set students work with.

After the Lesson: Have students determine how they will sort the letters.

Large Uppercase Letter Cards

A	B
C	D
E	F

Large Uppercase Letter Cards *(cont.)*

G	H
I	J
K	L

Large Uppercase Letter Cards *(cont.)*

M	N
O	P
Q	R

Large Uppercase Letter Cards *(cont.)*

S	T
U	V
W	X

Large Uppercase Letter Cards *(cont.)*

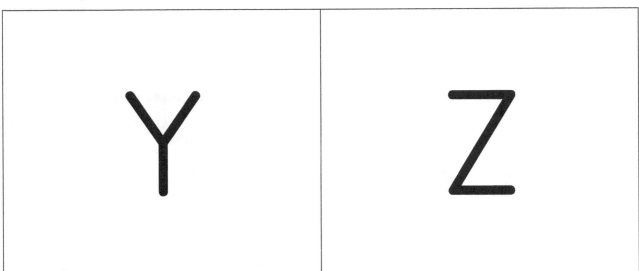

Large Lowercase Letter Cards

a

b

c

d

e

f

Large Lowercase Letter Cards *(cont.)*

g	h
i	j
k	l

Large Lowercase Letter Cards *(cont.)*

m	n
o	p
q	r

Large Lowercase Letter Cards *(cont.)*

s	t
u	v
w	x

Large Lowercase Letter Cards *(cont.)*

y	z

Blending with Cruising Cars

Objectives

- Know and apply grade-level phonics and word analysis skills in decoding words.
- Blend two or three phonemes into recognizable words.

Background Information

Knowledge of letters and sounds are building blocks for reading. Although it may still be a few years away for young students, the goal is fluent reading and comprehension. It is important that students begin working with both letters and sounds so they see and practice the connection of letters and sounds to reading. In Blending with Cruising Cars, students practice blending phonemes to read words with three or more phonemes using toy cars. Students need many opportunities to practice blending sounds into a word.

Materials

- small toy cars
- *Cruising Cars: Three Boxes* (page 80)
- *Cruising Cars: Four Boxes* (page 81)

Process

1. Prepare Cruising Cars mats. Make copies of *Cruising Cars: Three Boxes* on cardstock and place them in sheet protectors. This protects the mats as they are reused.

2. Choose a CVC word for students to decode, e.g., *bit*. Using an erasable marker, write one letter in each box on the Cruising Car mats.

3. Distribute the mats and toy cars to students.

4. Model how to say the individual sounds in the word and slowly push the car from the first box to the last box, one sound per box, for example: /b/ /ĭ/ /t/. Then, run the car along the road as you blend the sounds together to say the word, *bit*. Have students repeat your actions.

5. Repeat the process using other CVC words.

6. Once students are very comfortable blending CVC words, provide them with *Cruising Cars: Four Boxes* and use words with consonant blends.

Differentiation

During the Lesson: Assist any student who is having difficulty by placing your hand on top of their hand and controlling the car as it is pushed from one square to the next. Make *Cruising Cars: Four Boxes* available for students who are ready to blend consonant-consonant-vowel-consonant (CCVC) words. You may wish to copy *Cruising Cars: Four Boxes* onto the back of *Cruising Cars: Three Boxes*.

After the Lesson: Write CVC or CCVC words on cards. Place the word cards and toy cars in a basket and make them available for students to practice during center time.

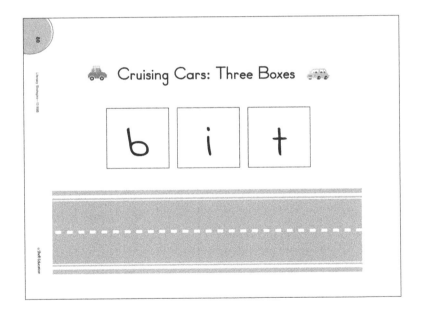

Cruising Cars: Three Boxes

b i t

Cruising Cars: Three Boxes

Cruising Cars: Four Boxes

High-Frequency Word Match

Objectives

- Know and apply grade-level phonics and word analysis skills in decoding words both in isolation and in text.
- Read common high-frequency words by sight.

Background Information

This strategy reinforces sound-symbol correspondence and provides opportunities for students to gain sight recognition of high-frequency words. Sight recognition of words is a key component in literacy instruction for beginning readers. The more automaticity a reader has, the less time they spend on the cognitive processes of decoding words and the more time they can spend on comprehension and meaning (Duke and Mesmer 2018; Ehri 1995, 1998, 2014). This strategy engages students in working with high-frequency words that have a one-to-one sound-symbol correspondence. The goal is to learn common high-frequency words to a level of automaticity.

Materials

- index cards

Process

1. Select high-frequency words with regular spellings (see the chart on page 83). Begin with words with one or two letters and build to words with three letters.
2. Neatly write the high-frequency words on index cards. Make two cards for each word.
3. Distribute the cards to students so that each student gets one card. Have students read the word on their cards.
4. Students keep their words to themselves until the teacher says, "Go!" Then, children hold the cards under their chins, facing out.
5. Direct students to look at the words their classmates have and find the classmate with the matching word.
6. Have each pair of students read their word together, sound by sound, and then blend each sound together to read the word. Then, have them trace the letters of the word with their fingers as they spell the word.
7. Collect and shuffle the high-frequency word cards and repeat the process.
8. Replace or add to the cards as often as desired.

Differentiation

During the Lesson: Differentiate the words given to students to ensure rigor for all students.

After the Lesson: Students at centers can play a matching game by placing all the cards face down and taking turns turning over two cards at a time to find the sets of words. The cards may also be used for student practice tracing the letters. You may wish to prepare the cards by tracing each letter with white glue and letting the glue dry before students use them to trace the words.

Words with One-to-One Sound/Symbol Correspondence

One-Letter Words	Two-Letter Words	Three-Letter Words
a	am	and
I	an	but
	at	can
	if	did
	in	get
	it	had
	no	has
	on	him
	up	his
		its
		not

Reading Comprehension and Content Knowledge

The strategies in this section correspond with key competencies identified in *What the Science of Reading Says about Reading Comprehension and Content Knowledge* (Jump and Kopp 2023). These research-based instructional strategies will help teachers bridge the gap between the science of literacy instruction and classroom practice.

Strategy	Skills and Understandings Addressed				
	Building Content Knowledge	Vocabulary	Language Structures: Syntax and Semantics	Text Structures and Verbal Reasoning	Literacy Knowledge: Print Concepts for Genre Studies
Using Text Sets for Wide and Extensive Reading	▓				
Creating Concept Maps	▓				
What I Know	▓				
Shared Experience	▓				
Explicit Vocabulary Word Instruction		▓			
Incidental Vocabulary Word Instruction		▓			
Shades of Meaning		▓			
Many Ways to Say It			▓		

Strategy	Skills and Understandings Addressed				
	Building Content Knowledge	Vocabulary	Language Structures: Syntax and Semantics	Text Structures and Verbal Reasoning	Literacy Knowledge: Print Concepts for Genre Studies
Identifying Multiple-Meaning Words			▓		
Picture Inference				▓	
Figurative Language Awareness				▓	
Teaching Concepts of Print					▓
Informational Text Genre Study					▓

Reading Comprehension and Content Knowledge

Simply put, reading comprehension is understanding what we read. It is the knowledge that words represent thoughts and ideas. It is the skill required for meaning-making, and meaning-making is the very heart of reading. Why read words if we cannot make meaning from them? While we may be able to define reading comprehension simply, the act is not so simple. Researchers from a variety of disciplines have attempted to describe, visualize, theorize, and model the processes that occur in a reader's mind when making meaning from words, and while there may not be a definitive model, there is much we have learned that has significant implications for instructional practices.

In order to comprehend what they read, readers must have strong foundational skills. They must have the ability to accurately and effortlessly decode most or all of the words in a text (Duke, Ward, and Pearson 2021). While decoding and fluency skills are necessary components for reading comprehension, they are not sufficient. Children need help developing and activating content knowledge and understanding new vocabulary. They also need to become familiar with print concepts, genres (fiction and nonfiction), syntax and semantics, and some aspects of text structure. Teachers can model and encourage specific actions that support students in the acquisition of the skills needed.

> Readers must be able to cognitively process the words, drawing meaning from their own knowledge and experiences to understand the author's message.

We know readers must be able to cognitively process the words, drawing meaning from their own knowledge and experiences to understand an author's message. Reading is a dialogue between the reader and the author, and during this dialogue, the reader generates questions to help anticipate meaning, search for information, respond intellectually and emotionally, and infer ideas from and explain further the content of the text. Young children need to be shown how to do this. And since fluency can influence comprehension, fluent reading must be modeled for children. Using voice modulation, demonstrating phrasing, applying punctuation appropriately, and emphasizing key words are all components of *prosody*, which means reading with expression. A fluent reader is a reader who is understanding what they read. Understanding the words in the text—the vocabulary—impacts both fluency and comprehension, which is why teachers must explicitly introduce vocabulary words and use appropriate intonation during shared reading activities. At this stage, children are still making connections between spoken words, written words, pictures or symbols, and objects or concepts they represent. Calling attention to these words while using gestures, pointing to a picture, or offering an explanation supports children's meaning-making and provides critical information that forms the basis of their background knowledge.

What Is Vocabulary?

What comes to mind when you hear the word *vocabulary*? Vocabulary knowledge plays an integral role in children's ability to comprehend reading material that is shared with them. Students with wider vocabularies find it easier to comprehend texts than do students with limited vocabularies. Moreover, students who have strong vocabularies have less difficulty learning unfamiliar words because those words are more likely to be related to words that they already know (Rupley, Logan, and Nichols 1999).

> Students who have strong vocabularies have less difficulty learning unfamiliar words because those words are more likely to be related to words that they already know (Rupley, Logan, and Nichols 1999).

Young learners need repeated exposure to new words and explicit definitions of those words, including descriptions of the function of the object being described or an explicit connection to pictures or props (Wasik and Hindman 2020). Young children first learn language, then they learn *through* language, and finally, they learn *about* language (Halliday 2004, 308). Young children are starting to use language to learn. That is, understanding that a word represents an object or idea, even if they have no exposure or experience with that object or idea. Language becomes the vehicle for introducing children to new concepts. Children may never have seen a camel or a lion in person, but through pictures and descriptions, they can learn to differentiate a camel from a lion by recognizing and labeling the specific characteristics of each. By having students practice using language to learn about ideas, educators are laying a foundation for deeper levels of word learning in the future.

Academic Vocabulary

General academic vocabulary refers to foundational words that cross multiple domains, such as *explain*, *discuss*, or *describe*. Modeling how to use complete sentences, and asking children to respond using these academic terms, increases their flexibility and fluency with these key words. This language becomes the entry point for learning about new things through language. When children grasp how to *describe* or *explain*, they expand their understandings that words carry meaning, offer direction, and provide clarity. Moreover, these words have high utility, which is why they are treated with importance in school.

Just as important is *domain-specific vocabulary,* or words that are specific to a subject. For example, *nocturnal* is a word that describes a very specific type of animal or insect. It is not an everyday word in the sense that it is common in daily conversation, but it is a word that provides a specific definition and description, which allows a child to make a distinction between types of animals, and it provides a means for categorizing and connecting learned information. Research shows that a word's meaning is contextualized within a network of larger understandings (Fitzgerald et al. 2020). It follows that the greater the store of a child's background knowledge, the more context will be available for retrieval of information. Recognizing a domain-specific term within a larger context allows a child to attach multiple layers of meaning to the term, strengthening connected ideas and deepening understanding. Jill Fitzgerald and her colleagues provide insight: "Larger mental networks (as compared to smaller networks) may be more supportive of students' vocabulary learning in general, and domain-specific learning in particular, because they more likely provide enriched, deeper, or more nuanced meaning associations for knowing a focal word" (2020, 858–859).

> The goal is to move new vocabulary into the established level for students so they can use the words in their own speech and writing.

Researchers categorize knowledge of words by three levels—unknown, acquainted, and established (Lapp, Flood, and Farnan 2008; Ryder and Graves 2003). *Unknown words* are words students neither recognize nor understand. *Acquainted words* are ones that students may recognize but must consciously think about to determine their meanings. *Established words* are those words that students recognize and can define easily and automatically. The goal is to move new vocabulary into the established level for students so they can use the words in their own speech and writing. It is not enough for students to be acquainted with the word *artifacts*—students need to use the term easily when speaking and writing. To achieve this, teachers must expose students to new words a number of times and in a variety of contexts. "With appropriate guidance and support, children's oral language will develop as they begin to use more complex grammar and vocabulary" (Brown 2014, 43).

Print Concepts and Foundational Skills

While vocabulary knowledge plays a critical role in reading comprehension (Cromley and Azevedo 2007; Perfetti and Stafura 2014), text features and print concepts provide additional context for navigating various text types. Recognizing that in English, words progress from left to right and from top to bottom makes reading a more predictable activity. Children see that they can glean information from text if they start at the beginning of a passage and read through to the end. Reading is not a scavenger hunt, it is a process of making meaning from an orderly display of information. During shared reading, moving your finger under the words as you read to children reinforces the left-to-right, top-down pattern. Showing how to turn the pages from the right side to the left side demonstrates book handling skills. Children learn to anticipate when text will continue versus when it will end, which reinforces their familiarity with story structures. Page numbers and headings become valuable reference points for retrieving information or keeping track of progress through a text.

Teachers must explicitly call attention to print, commenting on it, asking questions about it, and demonstrating the physical steps involved in handling books and reading (Justice and Sofka 2010). Use a pointer with a Big Book during read-alouds to distinguish text features. Pause under each word in a sentence, and call attention to the spaces between words, the punctuation marks, or the capital and lowercase letters. This shows children that the text is carefully constructed to convey one thought or idea at a time. The features of print become guideposts, helping identify when to stop or start a sentence, how to attribute speech to one character or another, and how to differentiate the beginning, middle, and end of a story. In fact, "all elements of a book's design communicate meaning and warrant attention" (Zucker, Ward, and Justice 2009, 68). For example, fonts and colors indicate moods and expressions. Captions under illustrations and photographs provide clarification. Speech bubbles and callouts link words and sentences to characters or characteristics, underscoring that words provide labels and descriptions. All these features of text should be pointed out and discussed with children while reading together to get them in the habit of looking at all aspects of a page and understanding that every facet of text is intentional and there for a reason, and so can impact understanding.

Language Structures: Syntax and Semantics

Comprehension is an incremental process—a series of encounters with text that leads to deeper understanding. Language structures provide the roadmaps that will help children navigate through a reading task. Beyond recognizing print features, such as headings or titles, children need to understand syntax. *Syntax* is the system of how words are arranged to make sense in a language. Syntactical knowledge includes an understanding of the functions of words and the rules of grammar that govern word arrangement, impacting and conveying meaning in a sentence, such as how a sentence works, what a pronoun stands for, and how connective words serve to combine ideas. For young children, rhymes and repetitive phrases help embed an understanding of syntax on a basic level. Rhymes help children predict words based on their sounds, and on their relationship to each other in the context of the poem or story. Repetitive phrases impact fluency and prosody by allowing children to practice intonation multiple times. "The repeated exposure of the words and word patterns allows students to store the information in their memory to use for other texts" (Zavala and Cuevas 2019, 66). Even the nonsense words found in some books show children the playfulness of language and demonstrate how words express feelings or describe situations. Zavala and Cuevas note, "This approach in using rhyming poetry to teach fluency is a more engaging way to keep students focused on the pattern" (2019, 68). Introduce syntax using chants, singing songs, and during read-alouds. Consider a story book that has repetitive phrases and sentence patterns, such as Margaret Wise Brown's *Goodnight Moon* (1947). Children may

> Comprehension is an incremental process—a series of encounters with text that leads to deeper understanding. Language structures provide the roadmaps that will help children navigate through a reading task.

start to predict the syntax, even when it becomes more complex: "Goodnight cow jumping over the moon. Goodnight light, and the red balloon." This process is a precursor to using academic language frames, which help older students construct complex sentences.

Semantics refers to the overall meaning of a sentence or the message the words convey. An essential part of semantic knowledge involves knowing how to determine the differences between words that convey similar meanings and understanding how these differences affect meaning, for example understanding how the use of the word *jog* as opposed to *run* changes the meaning of the sentence.

This understanding of the structure of language helps readers process and understand text at the sentence level. If decoding words is the foundation for learning to read words, semantics is the foundation for learning to comprehend the meaning of words. Semantic activities include showing connections between words, highlighting synonyms and antonyms, and explaining the meaning of unfamiliar words within the context of the story or narrative. Consider how one word, such as *plant*, may refer to a factory, to something found in a garden, or to something a person does. If students have only encountered this word in the context of gardening, they will need an explanation of how it also represents a building where manufacturing takes place. The more exposure children have to multiple meanings of words in different contexts, the broader their ability to go beyond decoding to map words to other concepts, which supports comprehension.

Text Structures and Verbal Reasoning

It is important that children are exposed to fiction and nonfiction, as knowledge of both genres supports reading comprehension. Nonfiction or informational texts may also support the expansion of young children's established vocabularies: "Exposure to and understanding of new vocabulary is one reason for reading informational texts as it exposes the reader to new content and opportunities to gain new knowledge" (Hall and Sabey 2007, 262). In addition, exposure to nonfiction texts supports comprehension skills: "Interactions around informational texts may provide opportunities for children to work on comprehending text meanings" (Dooley 2011, 178). Nonfiction text uses predictable text structures. These include description, compare-and-contrast, problem-and-solution, cause-and-effect, and sequence. Informational text may contain more than one text structure at a time, which can be particularly challenging for a developing reader. Explicit instruction helps children identify and understand the purpose of different text structures. Children need multiple experiences and exposures to a variety of informational text. It is also important to identify features of nonfiction text, such as tables, charts, captions, headings, and words in bold print. Show how these features aid in comprehension by calling attention to them and asking children to use the features to make predictions about the content.

To improve children's meaning-making acumen, they should be exposed to a variety of text genres. Multimodal text experiences, including digital texts, picture books, and interactive texts, support the construction of meaning. Fiction text in the form of picture books or narratives provides complex structures that may help expand children's ability to form intertextual connections. For example, a picture book may present multiple viewpoints through different characters, or it may unfold in a nonsequential order. Caitlin Dooley notes, "Postmodern children's literature presents unique opportunities for children's responses because of its complexity" (2011, 177). According to Dooley, children use pictures to create a narrative structure, and multiple readings will increase the "depth and dimension" of their understanding of the story (177). This kind of verbal reasoning is strengthened by interactive conversations around text.

> To improve children's meaning-making acumen, they should be exposed to a variety of text genres. Multimodal text experiences, including digital texts, picture books, and interactive texts, support the construction of meaning.

Reading Comprehension

Talking with children is the entry point for comprehension. In fact, studies show that "emergent comprehension is a learning process that occurs prior to (and during) beginning conventional reading" (Dooley 2011, 180). Media also aids in the meaning-making ability of young children. Dooley explains that "elements of comprehension stem from interactions with texts, such as storybooks, song charts, and computer games, prior to conventional print reading. From early interactions children develop knowledge about how to comprehend in ways that are essential to conventional reading comprehension development" (2010, 120). Talking with children while reading aloud models how to delve into a book, look at pictures for additional information and details, and notice the progression from beginning to middle to end.

Decades of research have helped us to determine what effective readers do as they read (NRP 2000). Proficient readers draw from their prior knowledge to predict events and information, generate hypotheses as they read, and determine the meaning of unknown words or confusing phrases. They make inferences, make connections between ideas and texts, draw conclusions, and summarize. These readers ask themselves questions throughout the reading process. To summarize these behaviors in one sentence, *proficient readers are strategic readers.*

These are not inherent skills. Children need modeling from adults to understand that a book is a tool, and then they need to be explicitly shown how to use the elements of a book to unlock meaning. According to Timothy Shanahan, "Strategies like monitoring, self-questioning, visualizing, comparing the text with prior knowledge, identifying text organization, and so on are all intentional, purposeful actions that are effective in improving comprehension or recall" (2018c, para. 7). Teaching the following strategies to students has been shown to increase reading comprehension: activating background knowledge, making predictions, making inferences, visualizing, identifying text organization, generating questions, summarizing, and monitoring comprehension (Shanahan et al. 2010). Strategy instruction is an important part of teaching reading in the elementary grades. Educators can lay a foundation of curiosity by modeling how to engage with the text. Purposeful talk adds to children's background knowledge and introduces new vocabulary words, helping children make associations to things they already know. Model how to ask questions about the text, and encourage children to make their own inquiries. Show how the pictures provide clues and help learners make predictions about what will happen next. Ask children to imagine the setting or paint a picture with their imagination. Inquire what they think the character is feeling, and show how the character's facial features or posture, the colors on the page, or the setting can support their inferences. Have children retell the story or remind them about this story when reading another story, so they can practice summarizing and making intertextual connections. These conversations do not need to be formal or structured. Having fun interactions with text will encourage children to practice these habits on their own and will support the use of structured reading strategies they will encounter when they enter school.

> Strategy instruction is an important part of teaching reading in the elementary grades. Educators can lay a foundation of curiosity by modeling how to engage with the text.

Content Knowledge

Decades of reading research have shown us that along with decoding and fluency skills, another key to reading comprehension is the development of a broad base of knowledge readers can activate and apply to the reading situation. This knowledge includes topics such as academic vocabulary, morphology, and familiarity with text and language structures, but it also includes topical knowledge. Wattenberg points out that "as students age and gain basic skills, the lack of knowledge typically becomes the much greater obstacle to good reading" (2016, 2). For young children, books are a doorway to knowledge and a window to a world beyond their immediate scope.

Current state standards have shifted the focus at the elementary grades from fiction to informational text. A broad base of content or topical knowledge can give readers a comprehension advantage when they encounter a diversity of topics, particularly in science and social studies. Having schema (relevant prior knowledge) for a topic aids in the comprehension process, and also in the learning process (Smith et al. 2021). When a topic or concept is introduced in text and students can initiate the retrieval process (activating their schema for the topic), they have an anchor to which they can connect the new information to better understand it (Anderson and Pearson 1984). Think of our schema as a set of folders in a filing cabinet (or in our "cloud storage"):

> When students have knowledge of facts, ideas, and concepts across content areas, they can develop an understanding of how concepts/topics are related, how they are explained, how processes work, and more.

it is easier for us to add items to our existing folders than it is to create a whole new folder with a whole new label and find things to fill it with. This is an overly simplistic but helpful analogy for thinking about the importance of schema. The advantage this broad knowledge bestows goes beyond the facts and information of a topic. When students have knowledge of facts, ideas, and concepts across content areas, they can develop an understanding of how concepts/topics are related, how they are explained, how processes work, and more. This familiarity can be transferred to new topics and content to facilitate learning.

Content and concept knowledge can support incidental word learning. When students have knowledge of a concept or topic, that information allows them to better understand new vocabulary or technical vocabulary related to that concept. This knowledge of related words can activate broader semantic networks (the organization of facts and knowledge in the mind) to enhance comprehension and accelerate new learning (Cervetti, Wright, and Hwang 2016; Willingham 2006). Concept and content knowledge will also assist readers in understanding words with multiple meanings. For example, exposure to and broad knowledge of marine life can help a reader distinguish the differing meanings of the word *school*, as in a *school of fish* as opposed to an *elementary school*. Similarly, familiarity with a topic can help students understand figurative language, distinguish that a statement is indeed figurative and not literal, and interpret the meaning of the figurative statement. For example, students read that a team of scientists really "hit it out of the park" with the results of their latest study. Exposure to or familiarity with baseball would help these students understand (1) that this is a figurative statement—that the scientists did not actually hit anything, and an actual park was not involved—and (2) that their results were significant and considered remarkable.

The recognition of the importance of building a broad base of content knowledge is part of the push for an increase in the amount of informational text students engage with during elementary school. Informational text also allows for instruction in different genres and text structures, furthering students' knowledge of organizational patterns, language structures, and knowledge across domains. To support building a strong base of content knowledge, teachers can implement thematic teaching—a method in which a theme or topic is used as a central focus for learning in a classroom. Thematic units create opportunities for students to develop and deepen content knowledge, learn vocabulary, and develop the language comprehension skills identified in Scarborough's Reading Rope (page 3). Thematic units allow for content to be covered across the curriculum, helping students make connections between concepts and ideas in different content areas.

Benefits of a Thematic or Topic-Based Unit

- Provides a teaching focus

- Integrates lessons across content areas

- Engages students in a topic of interest

- Draws on students' experiences and prior knowledge

- Builds students' knowledge on a topic

- Provides opportunities for students to make connections

- Develops vocabulary

- Makes planning more efficient

- It is fun!

The comprehension strategies presented in this section can all be used as part of thematic or topical units. Throughout the strategies, many examples are crafted around the thematic unit "bugs," demonstrating how content and lessons can be integrated around a theme.

Putting It All Together

The strategies in this section are intended to support the development of competent, independent, strategic readers who can understand and learn from a diversity of texts across a wide variety of topics. Educators can introduce new vocabulary that spurs the growth of children's background knowledge. Teachers can use read-alouds to show how to handle books, how sentences work, and how words can have multiple meanings depending on the context in which they are used. Combining informational text with fiction, and including digital texts, graphics, and media, supports children's comprehension by demonstrating how text structures cross genres. It is incumbent upon educators to explicitly introduce these elements to prepare students for reading, but equally important is to bring a playful attitude to reading. Ensuring that children interact with books in positive ways will encourage them as they continue on the road to reading.

Using Text Sets for Wide and Extensive Reading

Objectives

- Build and activate prior knowledge related to information and events in texts.
- Actively engage in group reading activities with purpose and understanding.
- Use illustrations and context to make predictions about text.

Background Information

Background knowledge is one of the pieces of the Language Comprehension strand of Scarborough's Reading Rope (2001). By activating and building background knowledge, teachers support students' abilities to engage with and comprehend texts. Text sets offer a concrete way for students to learn more about a topic of study. They provide the variety necessary for students to engage in wide and extensive reading using many types of texts across different genres. This kind of exposure helps students understand that topics can be written about in a variety of ways. Gathering a text set allows for both wide and extensive reading to happen throughout a thematic or topic-based unit.

Materials

- a variety of texts on a topic
- realia related to the topic

Process

1. Identify a topic or theme that will be the focus of study.
2. Gather texts around the chosen topic or theme. Use the following guidelines when selecting texts:
   - Vary genre and be sure to include fiction, nonfiction, poetry, songs, maps, and so on.
   - Vary reading level and be sure to include decodable texts, picture books, and wordless picture books.
3. Create an inviting display that is accessible to students. Surround the texts with other realia that help frame the topic or theme. For example, if the topic of the text set is *plants*, display a small shovel and seed packets near the books.

4. Introduce the display to students and explain that the class will be using the books to learn more about a topic. Read the titles of some of the books to students and ask what they have in common. Help students identify the topic the class will be studying. Provide students with a learning target or overarching question to guide their study using the text collection.

5. Read one of the texts to students as an introduction to the unit. Before reading, discuss the parts of a book (front cover, back cover, spine), and identify the author and illustrator.

6. Build background and vocabulary knowledge by reading a variety of books from the text set to students over the course of the unit of study.

   • During a unit, engage students in comparing and contrasting two texts to identify similar and different information learned from the texts.

   • After introducing a specific text, encourage students to return to it. For example, write the words to a song on chart paper. Display the chart and provide students with pointers. Encourage students to sing the song while pointing to the words on the chart.

Differentiation

Ensure that students can find books to learn from without reading (high-quality picture books or audio texts, for example). Provide students with a variety of ways to record their learning from the text collection.

Example Text Set for a Unit on Bugs

Fiction

The Very Hungry Caterpillar by Eric Carle

The Ants Who Couldn't Dance by Susan Rich Brooke

Ten Wriggly, Wiggly Caterpillars by Debbie Tarbett

I Am a Bee by Rebecca and James McDonald

In the Tall, Tall Grass by Denise Fleming

I Love Bugs! by Philemon Sturges

Nonfiction

Small But Mighty: All About Insects by Natalie Gagnon

Waiting for Wings by Lois Ehlert

Bugs A to Z by Caroline Lawton

The Bug Book by Sue Fliess

Bugs Are Insects by Anne Rockwell

Poems

"To an Insect" by Oliver Wendell Holmes

"The Bee" by Emily Dickinson

"The Humble-Bee" by Ralph Waldo Emerson

Creating Concept Maps

Objectives

- Build and activate prior knowledge related to information and events in texts.
- With prompting and support, identify the main topic and retell key details of a text.
- With prompting and support, identify basic similarities in and differences between two texts on the same topic (e.g., in illustrations, descriptions, or procedures).

Background Information

Concept maps are effective for visually organizing information related to concepts discussed in informational texts (Hattie 2009; Horton et al. 1993). Teachers can construct a concept map and present it to the class prior to reading or presenting new material to generate discussion around the topic and to build conceptual and word knowledge. In doing so, teachers better prepare students to understand what they are reading. The concept map can also be used after some initial exposure to the topic such as viewing a short video or examining an image or images related to the topic. Later, as students learn more about the topic, new ideas can be incorporated into the map.

Materials

- chart paper and markers

Process

1. Select a topic of study. Identify basic background information students need to know as they begin the unit. For example, if the topic is bugs, students may want to know the parts of a bug. Make a list of words or ideas.

2. Present the concepts to students as you draw and label them on chart paper. As you draw, define and explain concepts and vocabulary (see Basic Concept Map and Story on page 99). If drawing the images in front of students is challenging, consider doing a light sketch in pencil on the chart paper prior to the lesson and outlining the drawings with marker as you talk to students.

3. Invite students to share what they know about the topic.

4. Continue to add to the concept map as the unit of study continues and as students learn more about the topic through texts and other media. The initial concept map should provide basic background information that many students may already know. By the end of the unit, the concept map should include details learned throughout the unit.

Differentiation

During the Lesson: Provide students with blank sheets of paper and have them draw along with you as you share the information.

After the Lesson: Use the concept map as a source for students to practice creating sentences. For example, students can describe what they see, such as *The ants live in tunnels.*

Example Concept Maps for a Unit on Bugs

Basic Concept Map and Story

Insects are sometimes called bugs. They live all over the world. An insect can be very small, like a grain of rice, or big, like the length of a person's foot. An insect is a bug that has three body parts. [Draw a head, thorax, and abdomen.] Insects have six legs [draw six legs]. They have eyes on their heads [draw the eyes]. Some insects have eyes that look straight ahead and other insects' eyes are on the sides of their heads. Insects also have antenna on their heads [draw the antenna].

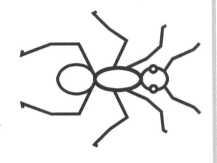

Adding to Concept Maps During a Unit

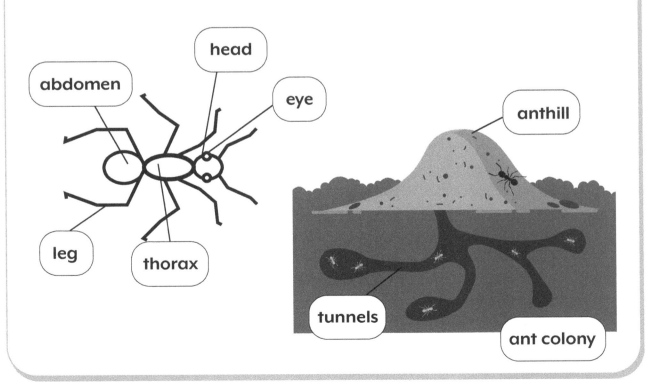

What I Know

Objectives

- Build and activate prior knowledge related to information and events in texts.
- Actively engage in group reading activities with purpose and understanding.
- Use illustrations and context to make predictions about text.

Background Information

The What I Know strategy activates students' background knowledge related to a topic. Background knowledge plays a vital role in reading comprehension, listening comprehension, and continued learning of concepts and ideas. The process of activating background knowledge supports building connections between what students already know and what is to be learned (Wilhelm, Fachler, and Bear 2019). This strategy is particularly useful when beginning a unit on a topic and can be used before reading any text. Prior to shared reading, teachers help students activate the background knowledge they have related to the topic or text. During reading, students explain how their experiences may relate to the topic or story. They also learn how their peers' experiences connect in similar or different ways.

Materials

- chart paper
- book to be read aloud

Process

1. Display the cover of the book that will be read so students can see it. Read the title, the author and illustrator names on the front cover, and any other important information on the cover. If the back cover has illustrations or text, display and discuss it.

2. Have students describe the photograph or illustration on the cover of the book. Encourage students to speak in complete sentences.

3. Tell students they may know things about the topic of the book, and it is important to think about those things while the book is being read. Explain that what they know about the topic may come from something they have experienced personally, something they have seen in another book, or something they have seen in videos, on TV, and so on.

4. Ask students to turn-and-talk to partners about what they already know about the topic. Tell students that it is okay if they do not know anything about the topic. That is why the class is reading the book—to learn more! Students may not be able to think

of anything right now, but as they hear their classmates talk, they may be reminded of something they do know.

5. Have students share connections they have to the topic. Record students' responses on chart paper. This can be scaffolded in several ways. For very young students, you can simply record the name of the student and add a simple drawing or short phrase. Or, a complete sentence can be recorded. Adjust how students' responses are recorded as needed.

6. Encourage students to make predictions about what you will read. List some predictions to check after reading.

7. While you are reading, stop periodically to allow students to think-pair-share on any background knowledge, connections, or predictions made with the text.

Differentiation

During the Lesson: Provide sentence starters or sentence frames for students to encourage a focus on the content of the output rather than sentence formation. For example, when describing the illustrations on the cover, encourage students to use the following sentence starter: *I see _____.*

After the Lesson: Repeating this activity in the middle of a unit of study allows students to make new connections and use newly learned information as background information, and provides a context for vocabulary to be used when speaking. This activity can also be used as an indicator of students' understanding of a topic and the possible need to address questions and misconceptions that arise.

Example Chart for a Book about Bugs

This three-column chart is based on *Hey, Little Ant* by Phillip and Hannah Hoose.

Text to self	Text to text	Text to world
I had ants in my house. My dad had to spray them. My sister tries to step on ants.	The ants go get food at picnics in *Hey, Little Ant* and in *One Hundred Hungry Ants.*	I know ants like to go in a line. Ants are very, very, very small.

Shared Experience

Objectives

- Build and activate prior knowledge related to information and events in texts.
- Use words and phrases acquired through conversations, reading and being read to, and responding to texts.
- Describe familiar people, places, things, and events and, with prompting, provide additional detail.

Background Information

A student's background knowledge plays an important role in reading comprehension (Anderson and Nagy 1992; Anderson and Pearson 1984; Neuman, Kaefer, and Pinkham 2014). In other words, the more a student knows about a topic, the more likely the student is to understand a text on the topic and thus learn more about the topic. We know that not all students come to the classroom with similar background experiences. Creating shared experiences provides a way to build background information and ensures everyone in the class has at least some exposure to the topic. Using carefully crafted experiences, teachers can build students' understanding of the topic and vocabulary in just a few minutes so that every student has some background knowledge to bring to the topic as new learning happens.

Materials

- sticky notes
- additional items as needed, depending on the exact shared experience

Process

1. Identify a shared activity students can participate in that will build a common knowledge base around a topic to be studied. Examples include the following:
   - Observe and describe an animal, the weather, an object from nature, and so on.
   - Examine a photograph or an illustration.
   - Watch a video.
   - Participate in an assembly or a field trip.
   - Conduct a science exploration or experiment.
   - Make a recipe.
   - Create an art project as a group.

2. Determine the background information and vocabulary you want students to gain from the experience. Record the information and vocabulary on sticky notes (or something similar) and keep them on hand during the activity as a reminder of the goals you want to accomplish.

3. Develop questions that will be used to prompt students throughout the activity. Record the questions and keep them easily accessible.

4. Guide students through the activity. Encourage them to generate as much of the desired language as possible. Add clarification and provide specific vocabulary as opportunities arise.

5. Make connections back to the activity as new information is learned during the unit of study.

Differentiation

During the Lesson: Provide sentence stems to assist students with generating sentences.

After the Lesson: Work together with students to generate and record several sentences describing the experience. Record the sentences on chart paper and display in the classroom.

Example of a Shared Experience for a Bugs Unit

Experience: Locate a place on the school campus that has ants, such as at the base of a tree. Take students on a walk to where the ants are located. Allow students to observe the ants.

Encourage students to describe what they are seeing.

- There is a whole bunch of ants.
- I see an ant with something big.
- The ants go fast.

Provide feedback to students' observations, rephrasing their sentences to add background information or vocabulary.

- Ants live in groups called colonies.
- The ants are marching in a line.
- Ants can carry objects much bigger than they are.

Ask questions to prompt students' observations.

- Where are the ants are going? Describe how they are walking.
- What do their bodies look like? Can you see sections on their bodies?

Explicit Vocabulary Word Instruction

Objectives

- Expand knowledge and use of a wide variety of words.
- With guidance and support from adults, explore word relationships and nuances in word meanings.
- Use words and phrases acquired through conversations, reading and being read to, and responding to texts.

Background Information

Instruction in vocabulary improves reading comprehension (Lehr, Osborn, and Hiebert 2004; NRP 2000). Isabel Beck, Margaret McKeown, and Linda Kucan (2013) describe three tiers of vocabulary that are useful when selecting words to teach (see the chart on page 105). They recommend providing robust instruction in Tier 2 words because these words have high utility and nuanced meanings. Picture books are an excellent source of Tier 2 words. Beck, McKeown, and Kucan suggest six words per week for explicit instruction for young students. Explicit vocabulary instruction should include the following: multiple exposures to the word, definition and context are provided for the word, and students are engaged with the word to help them process it. This strategy provides a routine for explicit word instruction that incorporates those recommendations.

Materials

- picture book to be read aloud
- illustration, photograph, or realia of the vocabulary words (*optional*)

Process

1. Preview a text you will read to students and identify five to six Tier 2 vocabulary words (see page 105) that you will introduce to students using explicit instruction.

   - Which words are students unlikely to know the meanings of?
   - Which words are likely to be used often in other contexts?
   - Which words require more explicit instruction due to nuanced meanings or other aspects? For example, students are more likely to require explicit instruction to understand the word *satisfy* than to understand the word *twirl*.

2. Select a word to introduce to students, for example the word *protect*. Introduce the word using the steps below at a quick pace. The whole routine should only take a few minutes. (See pages 106–107 for a detailed example of these steps.)

3. Say the word. Write the word on the board or display it so students can see it.

4. Clap or tap the syllables in the word; then have students clap the syllables with you.

5. Provide context for the word by using it in your own sentence or reading how it is used in a book.

6. Give an accurate, kid-friendly definition for the word. If possible, display an illustration, photograph, realia, or other representation of the word.

7. Discuss if the word sounds similar to another word or if there is an additional meaning for the word.

8. Have students interact with the word; for example, act out the word, create a hand gesture for the word, provide examples and non-examples, and so on. Have students repeat the word.

9. Plan for and provide intentional repeated exposure to the word over the following days.

Examples of Tiered Vocabulary for a Bugs Unit

Tier	Definition	Examples
Tier 1	Tier 1 words are heard daily in common communication, not content-specific words. Beck, McKeown, and Kucan (2013) identify Tier 1 words as general oral vocabulary words. These are words children will likely learn on their own.	ant, bee, bug, snail, ladybug, crawl, fly, egg, wing, head
Tier 2	Tier 2 words are more sophisticated. These words are often synonyms for Tier 1 words but show more nuance. They have high utility across many situations and disciplines. In fact, these words are often called "the language of books."	flutter, squirm, sting, cycle, section, protect, pair, bright, stage
Tier 3	These domain-specific vocabulary words are specific to a particular topic, subject, or concept. Tier 3 words are often found in bold print and in the glossary in nonfictional texts.	metamorphosis, chrysalis, larva, antennae, thorax, entomologist, exoskeleton

Example of Explicit Vocabulary Instruction

Step	Example
Say the word, emphasizing the stressed syllable.	pro**tect**
Write the word on the board or display it so students can see it.	protect
Clap or tap the syllables in the word.	Students would clap two times for the two syllables in protect. pro·tect
Provide context for the word by using it in your own sentence or reading how it is used in a book.	"A beetle has a hard shell on the outside of its body that protects its soft insides."
Give an accurate, kid-friendly definition for the word.	To protect means to keep away anything that would injure or hurt.
If possible, display an illustration, photograph, realia, or other representation of the word.	Show students a picture of a beetle and point out the hard outer shell on the beetle's body.
Discuss if the word sounds similar to another word or if there are multiple meanings for the word.	None for protect. For example, if the target vocabulary word is feast, distinguish feast from the word feet by ensuring students hear the /s/ in feast and by emphasizing that /s/ is not in feet. If the word has multiple meanings, acknowledge the other meanings.

Example of Explicit Vocabulary Instruction *(cont.)*

Step	Example
Have students interact with the word in some way.	**Act out the word**. For example, hold your hands up in front of your face as if you are protecting yourself from something being thrown at you. **Create a hand gesture** or movement that will be used when the word is referred to, for example, form one hand into a fist and cover it with the palm of the other hand. **Provide examples and non-examples** • You might *protect* a book by putting it high on a shelf so a baby will not get it and rip the pages. • If a little kid walks into the street, they are not *protected* from cars. • You wear sunscreen to *protect* your skin from the sun. **Ask questions about the word**. For example, *How do you* protect *yourself when you play a sport or ride a bike? How could you* protect *your eyes from the sun?*
Have students repeat the word.	*protect*

Differentiation

During the Lesson: Increase or decrease the number of words to teach based on observation as students interact with the words and begin to use the words in their oral language. For above-level support, point out and discuss the spelling of words.

After the Lesson: Have students orally produce sentences using sentence frames containing the word. For example, *I protect my toys from being broken by _____.*

Incidental Vocabulary Word Instruction

Objectives

- Expand knowledge and use of a wide variety of words.
- With guidance and support from adults, explore word relationships and nuances in word meanings.
- Use words and phrases acquired through conversations, reading and being read to, and responding to texts.

Background Information

In addition to explicit vocabulary instruction, there are incidental ways to intentionally expose students to vocabulary throughout the week. Clarification of some words can be provided near the point of use, as text is read to students (Beck, McKeown, and Kucan 2013). The goal of this strategy is to intentionally select words that can be taught incidentally. Incidental Vocabulary Word Instruction and Explicit Vocabulary Word Instruction (page 104) can both be used with the same picture book to support students' vocabulary development.

Materials

- picture book to be read aloud
- sticky notes

Process

1. Preview a text you will read to students and select several vocabulary words that can be introduced to students using incidental methods. The chart on page 109 has suggestions for quick and simple ways vocabulary can be demonstrated to students without providing more extensive and direct instruction. For example, *twirl* could be introduced quickly with a demonstration; students do not need a full vocabulary lesson to understand the meaning.

Incidental Instruction Methods	
Method	**Instruction**
Direct	Point to an image of the word in the illustrations. This works best with nouns.
Demonstrate	Use actions to demonstrate the word. This works best with verbs.
Define	Provide a quick definition of the word within the sentence.

2. Place sticky notes on the pages with the words as a reminder that you are going to provide incidental vocabulary instruction as you read that page.

3. When you read the book to students, as you come to the selected pages provide the incidental vocabulary instruction (see examples on page 110).

Differentiation

During the Lesson: Have students act out any words that you demonstrate. Taking a moment for this will help solidify the words for students.

After the Lesson: Provide opportunities for students to encounter the words repeatedly throughout the week by incorporating them into ways you interact with students. Encourage situations where students have an opportunity to use the words in oral language.

Example of Incidental Vocabulary Instruction

The following example is based on *All About Ants* by Jody Smith (Teacher Created Materials, 2024).

Demonstrate: Use your arm in a up and down motion in front of you to simulate a wave of water.

Ants cannot swim. But, if a wave of water comes, they can make a raft. They can be safe that way.

6

Most ants do not live too long. But some ants can live for as long as 30 years!

7

Direct: Use your finger to point to the raft of ants.

Define: Safe means where nothing will hurt them.

Shades of Meaning

Objectives

- With guidance and support from adults, explore word relationships and nuances in word meanings.

- Demonstrate understanding of frequently occurring verbs and adjectives by relating them to their opposites (antonyms).

- Use words and phrases acquired through conversations, reading and being read to, and responding to texts.

Background Information

Learning how words relate to other words is an important part of vocabulary development. When students compare words and develop awareness of nuances in word meanings, they gain a deeper and broader understanding of the words (Greenwood and Flanigan 2007). In Shades of Meaning, students work together to sort pictures showing gradients in meaning and then decide on labels for the pictures. Thinking about and discussing the shades of meaning enhances students' vocabularies and helps them see how words are connected.

Materials

- pictures showing examples of words in specific categories

Process

1. Identify a category of words to work with, for example *feelings*.

2. Think of opposites within the category, for example *happy* and *sad*.

3. List words with similar meanings to the words identified in step 2. Be sure to select words that students would likely encounter in text or everyday conversation with an adult. For example: *happy—joyful, excited; sad—gloomy, down.*

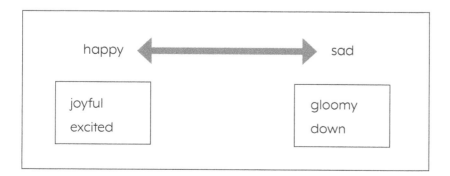

4. Over time, teach students the words using the routine for Explicit Vocabulary Word Instruction (page 104).

5. Display pictures showing examples of the words. Pictures can be found in magazines, on the internet, or in books.

6. Have students sort the pictures to show nuances or gradients in meaning, for example, from the person who is the "most happy" to the one who is the "most sad."

7. Have students work together to determine which word best matches each picture. Label the pictures.

Categories

size: large/small

temperature: hot/cold

movement: walk/run

state: awake/asleep

Differentiation

During the Lesson: Limit the number of words you introduce at one time, gradually increasing the quantity as students show they are able to work with more words.

After the Lesson: Provide students with picture books and ask them to find illustrations that match the category (e.g., pictures that show feelings), and share the examples with the class.

Example of Shades of Meaning During a Bugs Unit

This example shows size words that can be used to describe insects.

giant   large   big   medium   small   little   tiny

Many Ways to Say It

Objectives

- Use a combination of drawing, dictating, and writing to compose informative/explanatory texts in which they name what they are writing about and supply some information about the topic.
- Speak in complete sentences to describe familiar people, places, things, and events with prompting and support.

Background Information

Knowledge of sentence structure—how words and phrases are combined to make meaning—contributes to effective word reading and reading comprehension (Moats 2020b; Scarborough 2001). Young learners are just becoming aware of the power of words. Though they have begun speaking in sentences, they do not have a conscious awareness of the rules that govern how sentences are constructed in English. With this strategy, students manipulate the components of sentences and construct their own similar sentences. Helping students pull sentences apart and explore how the components interact with one another supports their understanding of text and develops language skills.

Materials

- informational text

Process

1. Write a topic as the title at the top of a sheet of chart paper (e.g., *Ants*). Create three columns below the title.

2. Preview the text. Label each column of the chart with a connecting word (a verb or linking verb) that can be used with information presented in the text (see example chart below).

Sample Text
Ants live in groups. Their home is a nest. Most nests are in holes, but they can be in other places, too. They can be huge, too. One ant nest is 13 miles long!

Ants		
live	have	can

3. Read the text aloud to students without stopping.

4. Introduce the chart to students and discuss the connecting words in each of the columns. Explain that as you read the text a second time, they will listen for information that can be added to the chart.

5. Reread the text aloud. While reading, stop occasionally and ask students if they heard any new information that can be added to the chart.

6. Record student responses on the chart. When adding information, reread the sentence where the information is found. Discuss how the sentence is constructed. Also, point out words that mean the same as one of the connecting words. For example, in the sample text, the reader learns that ants live in groups, nests, and holes; however only one sentence uses the word *live*: *Ants live in groups*. The author of the sample text uses other sentence structures and other words for *live* and connects ideas from one sentence to the next to convey places an ant lives.

Ants		
<u>live</u>	<u>have</u>	<u>can</u>
in groups	6 legs	lay eggs
in nests	antennae	carry heavy things
in holes		make paths
other places		

7. Continue to read the text and solicit ideas from students to complete the chart. Add sketches next to the words on the chart to support students.

8. Extend the learning by having students dictate a sentence from each column on the chart as you record their ideas. Build understanding of print concepts such as one-to-one correspondence of written and spoken words by pointing to the words as you read the sentences with the students.

Differentiation

During the Lesson: Challenge students to create their own sentences with the information from the chart by combining at least two ideas from the chart. For example, *Ants live in groups and can carry heavy things.* Students create more complex sentences when they are asked to combine ideas into one sentence.

After the Lesson: When students are familiar with this activity and have done it with several different texts, have them help determine the connecting words that will be listed at the top of the chart. This helps students think about the whole text and the main information the author conveys.

Identifying Multiple-Meaning Words

Objectives

- Determine or clarify the meaning of unknown and multiple-meaning words and phrases.
- Identify new meanings for familiar words and apply them accurately.

Background Information

Although students may know and use words with multiple meanings, they often have not thought about these words as having more than one meaning. Identifying words with multiple meanings encourages students to think metacognitively about their understanding of each word and the related concepts. The more exposure children have to multiple meanings of words in various contexts, the broader their ability to go beyond decoding to map words to other concepts, which supports comprehension.

Materials

- chart paper
- text

Process

1. Create a three-column table on a sheet of chart paper.

2. Read a text to students. Stop at words with multiple meanings as they are encountered in the text.

3. Name the word and explain that it has more than one meaning. Have students think of the various meanings of the word. If students are not familiar with the meanings, share them with students.

4. Write the words and their multiple meanings on the chart. If possible, draw pictures to show

Word	Meaning 1	Meaning 2
bat		
wave		
bark		
mouse		

the meanings of the words. If the meaning is difficult to illustrate, record a simple sentence using the word in context.

5. Reread the sentence in the text with the multiple-meaning word. Have students determine which meaning the author is using in the sentence.

6. Discuss how students know which meaning is intended. What other words in the sentence or sentences surrounding the word help the reader determine which meaning is intended? Are there picture clues that help support the meaning?

7. Continue reading the text and adding to the chart.

Multiple-Meaning Words	
mouse	chip
duck	fly
bark	leaves
can	bat
shower	kind
hard	trunk

Differentiation

During the Lesson: Use realia or images of multiple-meaning words to provide visual support for different meanings.

After the Lesson: Display the multiple-meaning word chart in the classroom. Encourage students to identify other words that have multiple meanings. Discuss the words and add them to the chart.

Example Using Text During a Bugs Unit

Sample Text:

Ants **_can_** lift things that are large for their size.

Ants cannot swim. But, if a **_wave_** of water comes, they find something to make into a raft to be safe.

Word	Meaning 1	Meaning 2
can	I can sing.	
wave		

Picture Inference

Objectives

- Activate prior knowledge related to the information and events in texts.
- Use illustrations and context to make predictions about text.

Background Information

With this strategy, students are guided through the process of making inferences about pictures, which is a step toward making inferences about texts. Research demonstrates that the ability to make inferences, or "read between the lines," is a predictor of reading comprehension (Elleman and Oslund 2019). Making inferences involves being able to draw connections between what an author states explicitly and the hidden meaning or understanding. Timothy Shanahan explains, "Authors don't tell everything. They imply an awful lot. Inferences are used to make sense of those implications" (2021, para. 9).

Materials

- a photograph or illustration

Process

1. Choose a photograph or illustration that is intriguing and lends itself to making inferences.

2. Show students the picture. If possible, mount it in the center of a sheet of chart paper so that you can write around the picture.

3. Tell students you want them to make observations about the picture by telling things they can point to and name in the picture. Label or list the things students name.

   - Accept only direct observations about what is in the picture and can directly be labeled.

4. After the labels have been added to the picture, tell students that an inference can be made using all the picture clues. Ask students to make inferences using prompts such as these:

   - Ask students what they think the people are doing. Have students tell why they think the people have gone grocery shopping. Ask what they might be going to do next.

   - Ask students how they know the people are not at a different place, such as a park.

   - Explain that there are clues in the picture that help us to understand what is happening, even though the picture does not show the people buying groceries. Discuss the clues.

cars

shirt

child

pineapple

shopping cart

groceries

Differentiation

During the Lesson: If students attempt to make an inference during the picture labeling part of the strategy, ask them to come up to the picture and point to what they want labeled. If they cannot point to it in the picture, it cannot be labeled. For example, if a student says the people are going home, ask them to come point to the home. Since there is not a home in the picture, it cannot be labeled. You may wish to say something like, "What a great inference! We will talk about inferences after we finish labeling our observations."

After the Lesson: Increase the rigor as students are ready by selecting pictures where the inference is less obvious or where more than one inference can be made. Discuss why and how more than one inference is possible.

Example of Picture Inference During a Bugs Unit

The following example is based on *Hey, Little Ant* by Phillip and Hannah Hoose (Tricycle Press, 1998).

Direct Observation of the Cover

The title of the book is *Hey, Little Ant*.

The ant is on a stick.

The child is wearing glasses.

The ant is smaller than the child.

The child is looking at the ant.

The ant is looking at the child.

The ant is standing with its arms raised.

Inferences

The child is talking to the ant.
The ant is talking to the child.

Figurative Language Awareness

Objective

- With prompting and support, ask and answer questions about unknown and multiple-meaning words and phrases.

Background Information

Figurative language refers to a use of words that diverges from their literal meanings. When students encounter language that does not mean what it says, they may miss important information and lack full comprehension. The idea of figurative language itself, as well as specific figures of speech, can be explicitly taught to young students. The main goal in working with figures of speech is exposure to the idea and building awareness of how authors use figures of speech to help tell stories and express ideas. Discussing figurative language as students experience it in literary and informational text is an effective approach.

Materials

- literary and informational texts
- chart paper

Process

1. Choose one or two examples of figures of speech to raise students' awareness of this type of language (e.g., *hold your horses*, *blanket of snow*). Share these with the class and discuss their meaning. Help students understand that these phrases mean something other than the exact words. Explain that people often use phrases like this when they want to make a point or express their ideas more strongly.

Idioms Related to Bugs

Their child is a social butterfly.

The baby looked snug as a bug in a rug.

The students were busy as bees.

He had butterflies in his stomach.

I'd like to be a fly on the wall.

She made a beeline for the dessert.

Don't be a litterbug.

She's sick with a bug.

The baby was as cute as a bug.

Let me put a bug in your ear.

He is a bookworm.

You opened a can of worms.

The classroom was a hive of activity.

I have a bee in my bonnet.

2. Create a chart to record instances of figurative language. As the class reads books and encounters various figures of speech, pause to discuss them. Record them on the chart and discuss how the author is using them to help explain, make a point, or exaggerate.

3. Introduce students to additional examples of figures of speech that are age appropriate, even if text examples cannot be found.

Differentiation

During the Lesson: Encourage students to try to use the context of the text or illustrations to help figure out what the figurative language means.

After the Lesson: Weave the figurative language found in texts into instruction throughout the course of a week so students are exposed to it several times in a short period of time.

Figurative Language Awareness During a Bugs Unit

Type	Definition	Example
hyperbole	exaggeration	The people looked as **small as ants** from the airplane.
idiom	non-literal phrase	Do you have **ants in your pants**?
metaphor	implied comparison between two things	It really **bugs** me when you chew with your mouth open.
personification	human characteristics expressed by non-human subjects	
simile	comparison using *like* or *as*	The server was **as busy as a bee**.

Teaching Concepts of Print

Objectives

- Identify the front cover, back cover, and title page of a book.
- Demonstrate understanding of the organization and basic features of print.
- Follow words from left to right, top to bottom, and page by page.

Background Information

Knowledge of print concepts influences children's language development, phonemic awareness, phonics, word reading, and reading and writing development (Hiebert et al. 1998; Morris 1993; Roberts 1992). While many children come to school with the understanding that print has meaning and an awareness of print conventions such as directionality, word boundaries, and punctuation, teachers need to explicitly teach these concepts to ensure that all students master them.

Materials

- Big Books

Process

1. Use a Big Book or larger book to ensure the book can be seen by all students.
2. Select one concept of print to teach at a time (see the chart on page 124). Provide explicit instruction on the concept of print, modeling and thinking aloud about how to interact with texts, including print books, digital materials, and text displayed in the classroom.
3. Continue to focus on one specific concept of print as you read books to students over an extended period of time until students are familiar with the concept.
4. Teach another concept of print, working on it for a period of time as you continue to review the first concept of print.

Differentiation

During the Lesson: Give individual or pairs of students copies of the book you will be reading. Together, walk the class or small groups through reading the book and practicing the concept of print being emphasized. If students are not yet able to read the words, they can tap the words as you tap-read them. Students may also echo read with you.

After the Lesson: Make the connection between reading and writing by encouraging students to leave a space between words when they write. Communicate with families about how to reinforce print concepts when reading at home.

Concepts of Print

Concept of Print	Explicit Teaching
How to hold a book	Model how to correctly hold a book. Teach that the words on the cover are facing upright and the binding of the book is on the left.
Reading from top to bottom/left to right	Explicitly model for students how to read words from left to right and from the top of the page to the bottom of the page.
Turning pages	Model how to turn the pages of a book by using the thumb and index finger and gently pulling on the top right corner of the page. Remind students to be gentle so the pages do not rip as they are being turned.
One-to-one word matching	Point to each word as you read it.
Spaces between words	Model the print awareness skill of how to notice the space between words when reading a text. Show that the words on the cover and on the inside pages have spaces between them.
Return sweep	Read all the words in a line, pointing to each word as you read it. Discuss where to continue reading when you get to the end of the line. Use your finger to model the return sweep, showing that you need to go to the beginning of the next line, without skipping lines.
Special text features	Identify any special features in the book you are reading such as the table of contents, glossary, headings, bold words, sidebars, captions, diagrams, charts, graphs, and maps. Tell students why the feature is included and explicitly teach how to use the feature.

Informational Text Genre Study

Objectives

- Actively engage in group reading activities with purpose and understanding.
- With prompting and support, describe the connection between two individuals, events, ideas, or pieces of information in a text.

Background Information

Reading widely introduces students to different genres, which supports reading comprehension. Knowing the features of different genres and understanding how they function aids students in comprehending what they read (Dewitz et al. 2020; Shanahan et al. 2010). To help build awareness of various genres, teachers of young students can begin by providing explicit instruction about the features and structures of informational text (Massey 2014).

Materials

- informational texts on the topic being studied (Big Books if possible)
- realia or props related to the topic

Process

1. Select one of the books to read and preview it with students. Read the title and have students look at the cover and predict what they think the book will be about. Engage students by sharing props or realia.

2. Read the book aloud, taking time to point out the features.

Informational Text	
Features	**Structures**
• about a specific topic or event • table of contents • headings • photographs and captions • diagrams	• cause and effect • compare and contrast • description • problem/solution • sequence of events

3. Think aloud to model how you identify one of the text structures used in the book. You may wish to identify signal words used in the book that indicate the text structure (see Common Signal Words on page 127). Keep in mind that informational books often use more than one text structure so, as students are ready, discuss additional text structures.

4. As the class continues the unit of study over the following days, read additional informational texts related to the topic. Point out features and text structures of each book.

5. After reading a few informational books, choose two of them and compare ways they are alike and different. Discuss the information presented, the features used, and text structures used.

6. Display the books so students can return to them on their own.

Differentiation

During the Lesson: Provide students with their own copies of the text. As the text structure is discussed, have students turn to the pages in the book that have the associated features.

After the Lesson: As students become more familiar with text structure, have them assist in determining the structure of a particular text.

Common Signal Words

Text Structure	Signal Words
cause-effect	as a result, because, brought about, consequently, if . . . then, is caused by, leads to, since, so, that is why, the effect of, when . . . then
compare-contrast	also, although, as opposed to, as well as, both, but, different, however, like, not only . . . but also, on the other hand, same, similar(ly), too, yet
description	all, appears to be, for example, for instance, in front of, looks like, most(ly), some, specifically, such as, to illustrate, too
problem-solution	answer, challenge, conclusion, fortunately, led to, one challenge, problem, question, result, solved, trouble, unfortunately
sequence of events	after, before, during, eventually, finally, first, following, immediately, in the end, later, meanwhile, next, now, then, when, while

SECTION III:
Writing

The strategies in this section correspond with three domains of emergent writing that need to be addressed when teaching young children (Puranik and Lonigan 2014). These domains are conceptual knowledge, or young learners' awareness of the purpose and meaning of print; procedural knowledge, skills in the mechanics of writing; and generative knowledge, which refers to the ability to write to convey ideas.

Strategy	Skills and Understandings Addressed		
	Purpose and Meaning of Print	Mechanics of Writing	Writing to Convey Ideas
Print-Rich Environment	■	■	■
Multisensory Letter Formation Practice		■	
Name Writing	■	■	
Morning Message	■		
Picture Word Chart		■	■
Experience, Talk, Write			■
Journal Writing		■	■
Predictable Sentences			■
The Big Three			■

Writing

Writing, the act of composing and expressing ideas, opinions, and views in print, is a vital component of children's literacy development. Researchers Cynthia Puranik and Christopher Lonigan developed a framework that helps explain the emergent writing skills of young learners (2014). These skills are grouped according to three domains: conceptual knowledge, procedural knowledge, and generative knowledge.

- *Conceptual knowledge* involves learning that "writing has a purpose and that print is meaningful (i.e., it communicates ideas, stories, and facts)" (Byington and Kim 2017, 74). When young children recognize that the red sign with white letters on many street corners means *stop*, they are demonstrating conceptual knowledge that print and symbols carry meaning.

- *Procedural knowledge* refers to the mechanics of writing. Having children use magnetic letters, crayons, sidewalk chalk, finger paints, and peg boards promotes fine-motor skills and gives children practice crafting words and sentences, even if they are using invented spellings or nonsense combinations.

- *Generative knowledge* refers to the ability to write phrases or sentences that convey meaning. Early childhood teachers can help children compose stories, create lists, make labels, and share ideas.

As children develop skills in these domains, connecting writing to reading will encourage progress in both areas. Exposure to books and models of writing reinforces the development of emergent writing skills.

> "Knowledge of the principles, concepts, and functions of writing represent children's knowledge concerning the purposes and basic structure of writing. Knowledge of the alphabet, including identification of letters and the ability to write letters, name writing, and spelling of simple words represent children's knowledge and skills concerning the mechanics of writing. The ability to produce writing beyond the letter or word level represents an ability that is separate from the mechanics of writing." (Puranik and Lonigan 2014, 465)

Hope Gerde, Gary Bingham, and Barbara Wasik (2012) describe twelve research-based best practices for writing instruction in early childhood classrooms:

1. Build writing into your daily schedule.
2. Accept all forms of writing.
3. Explicitly model writing.
4. Scaffold children's writing.

5. Encourage children to read what they write.

6. Encourage invented spelling.

7. Make writing opportunities meaningful.

8. Have writing materials in all centers.

9. Display theme-related words in the writing center.

10. Engage in group writing experiences.

11. Make writing a way to connect with families.

12. Use technology to support writing.

Thoughtfully integrating these practices promotes children's writing development and provides a foundation for their emerging literacy skills.

Oral language development supports early writing ability: "variation in children's oral language skills (composed of vocabulary, grammatical knowledge, and sentence imitation) was positively related to writing for children at the end of kindergarten" (Kim et al. 2011, 11). Given that oral storytelling is a precursor to writing, encourage children to sing, talk, and share. For example, after children listen to a story, encourage them to tell or write one of their own. Have them mimic the sentence structures. Use songs and chants, and have children use body movements to support sequencing skills. Just like using their fingers to count, using their hands to "shake it all about" or their feet to "hop to the left" reinforces that words have meaning and that sentences tell us something, such as what to do or how to move.

The Role of Genre in Early Writing

Writing is a complex, cognitive, self-directed, goal-driven activity that communicates thoughts and ideas (Graham et al. 2012). As students progress through the elementary grades, writing should become an increasingly independent task. Students will learn to understand that writing serves a variety of purposes: arguing and persuading, conveying information, sharing an experience, or telling stories to entertain an audience. Each of these purposes reflects the various genres of writing. As young children are engaging with both fiction and nonfiction text, they can also recognize some of the features of different genres of writing. Then, they can mimic these components in their own expressive endeavors. Make sure to point out how pictures help tell a story, and model how to summarize the events to show beginning, middle, and end. Have children use these elements in a story of their choice, either in response to a book you read or about a topic of their own choosing. When children get to write for different purposes, and have some level of autonomy over their writing, both their motivation to write and their desire to improve increase. "In contrast to reading, a central component of motivation to write is interest in expressing one's feelings, ideas, and perceptions. In order to do so, one must maintain some artistic control and have the freedom to exercise one's imagination" (Nolen 2007, 245).

Narrative Writing

For early learners, narrative writing involves using "a combination of drawing, dictating, and writing to narrate a single event or several loosely linked events" (National Governors Association Center for Best Practices and Council of Chief State School Officers 2010, 19).

> When children get to write for different purposes, and have some level of autonomy over their writing, both their motivation to write and their desire to improve increase.

Narratives can be personal, relating events that happened to the child, or they can be fictional stories about made-up characters. Introducing narratives through picture books and read-alouds promotes dialogue and offers children an opportunity to hear multiple perspectives and viewpoints. Then, when they are asked to mimic a story, add to a narrative, or interpret the events described, they have a richer base to draw upon. Use mentor texts and highlight narrative elements while you read. Point out the characters, setting(s), and main points of the plot. Emphasize how the words and the pictures help show what is happening, and ask what might happen next, or what may have happened before. When writing their own narratives, each child can work independently, or each can contribute one page to a class book as part of a collaborative endeavor.

Opinion Writing

Opinion writing is the forerunner of persuasive writing, which is intended to convince or influence. Persuasive writing begins with a claim that is supported by different kinds of evidence, either selected from supporting texts or from personal experiences. Younger children can provide their opinions about events, places, topics, or ideas, and then be encouraged to explain why they think the way they do. This process will get them in the habit of justifying their thoughts and feelings to add weight to their opinions. Use opinion writing tasks to introduce academic vocabulary such as *because*, *since*, *best*, *worst*, *most*, or *least*. Encourage conversation between partners so they can hear other viewpoints and practice speaking and listening skills as they learn to agree or disagree politely.

Informational or Explanatory Writing

Informational writing requires children to name their topic and then provide information about it. For example, children can write about the members of their families, or describe their morning or nighttime routines. Informational writing blends nicely with content-area instruction, as it provides a way for children to demonstrate their understanding. Writing process steps for a classroom procedure (how to wash your hands), documenting how a chick hatches from an egg, or describing the significance of a holiday or special event are ways that children can practice writing that offers clear and concise explanations and information. Have them explain how addition works by writing a math sentence, complete with pictures, such as "Maya picked three dandelions, and Josh picked two dandelions. Together they picked five dandelions." Posting students' informational writing around the classroom gives them ownership of their environment and showcases their understanding of things they have learned.

Stages of Writing

When learning to write, young children move through several stages as their knowledge and skills develop. Teresa Byington and YaeBin Kim (2017) describe the following four general stages:

- **Awareness, Exploration, or Scribbling Stage**: Children create drawings that represent writing and make scribbles (including wavy scribbles) that they intend as writing.

- **Emergent or Experimental Writing Stage**: Children write letter-like forms using shapes, generally printing from left to right. Letter strings are common during this stage.

- **Transitional or Early Writing Stage**: Children leave spaces between groups of letters or letter-like symbols. They begin to write letters based on sounds. The first letter of the word or the beginning and ending sounds represent the full word.

- **Conventional Writing Stage**: Children write letters proficiently and spell their names and other words correctly. They use punctuation in sentences.

Providing children with daily opportunities to write in the classroom and honoring their efforts lays the foundation for ongoing development of their writing skills and knowledge.

The Writing Process

The writing process allows a writer to take a piece of writing from the beginning, the generation of ideas, to the end, producing a published work. For elementary students, this process includes planning, drafting, sharing, revising/editing, publishing, and reflection/evaluation. The writing process at the emergent writing level may include one or more of these steps, and is usually conducted as a group, though on occasion it is done individually. Employing a model of gradual release during writing instruction is an important part of developing independent writers. Young-Suk Kim and her colleagues found that "students who were successful were in environments that were scaffolded but also allowed them to work independently" (2011, 530).

Writing for meaning and expressing oneself to others is intricate and complex work. Using the writing process helps the writer take a piece of writing from the beginning, or brainstorming, to the end, or the published piece. There are different modifications to consider at each step of the writing process for emergent writers.

Prewriting

This is the phase during which all writing begins. At this stage, writers generate ideas, brainstorm topics, make connections, or talk and think about ideas. Emergent writers typically need to see pictures or engage in hands-on experiences, then have time to talk and share. For young learners, prewriting may consist of whole-group work, such as sharing opinions about favorite foods, examining pictures of a specific season and discussing its features, or labeling the parts of a bird. Then, children can dictate or tell a story about the bird, or provide information about the kind of weather experienced during the season, or describe which food is their favorite and why.

For younger children, prewriting includes:

- whole-class or small-group discussions
- realia, picture cards, or manipulatives
- tools like binoculars or magnifying glasses to help identify characteristics and details
- matching or sequencing activities

Drafting

At the drafting stage of the writing process, students begin to put their ideas on paper. Young children may need to use sentence frames or simple graphic organizers (e.g., for sequencing) to help them do this. Pictures and drawings are part of the composition. Teachers encourage students to write as much as they can on their own. Scribbling and invented spellings are developmentally appropriate in these early writing stages for young learners, and teachers can ask children to "read" their drafts aloud, and then provide scaffolds such as word cards or posters to help them transition to writing.

Drafting can include:

- oral rehearsal of what will be written
- putting pictures or drawings on paper
- working for a designated amount of time
- invented spelling

Revising/Editing

This phase of writing consists of two parts: revising looks at the organization and structure of the writing, while editing looks at the mechanics of the writing. Eventually, students must understand how to do both. When revising, students analyze their writing for the required traits: sequencing words in a step-by-step process, descriptive language in a fictional story, topic sentences and supporting details in a persuasive piece. For younger learners, revising can take place through retelling or sharing with the teacher, who asks questions about the content to support children in adding more to their written work. If children are ready, have them work with partners. The partners ask questions about what they hear, using the five "Ws"—who, what, where, when, why. Children can then add to their original piece to provide more elaboration.

Editing could simply mean having children use a short checklist to make sure their sentences start with capital letters, include spaces between words, and end with correct punctuation. Cathy Collier calls these "the Big 3," and provides a process for helping children learn to use them (2022).

Revising and editing might include:

- sharing the piece aloud with a partner or teacher
- adding missing information
- checking for use of capitalization, spacing, and punctuation
- deleting unnecessary, incorrect, or duplicate information
- checking for correct spelling

Publishing

Publishing allows students to write for an authentic audience and celebrate their hard work. It occurs after the other steps are completed and the student is ready to produce the final copy, which can be handwritten or typed. The goal is to present the written information attractively so others can enjoy it.

Publishing involves:

- creating a final copy
- adding illustrations, borders, a cover, and so on
- sharing orally
- publishing in a class book
- posting on a classroom website, a blog, a social media site, or another platform

Ensuring that students understand the purpose for crafting a piece of writing and the elements required, along with consistently providing students time to work through the process of writing, will allow them to hone their craft. As they develop as writers, they will become better at expressing their thoughts and ideas and will grow more comfortable with writing.

The Role of Grammar and Mechanics in Writing

According to the National Early Literacy Panel (NELP), the following skills are predictors of reading and school success: alphabet knowledge, phonological awareness, rapid automatic naming of letters or numbers, rapid automatic naming of objects or colors, writing or writing one's own name, and phonological memory (NELP 2008). As discussed previously, when students have a firm command of the foundations of reading (decoding and fluency), they can better attend to comprehension of a text. Similarly with writing, when foundational writing skills are in place, more time and attention can be spent on the craft of writing (Graham et al. 2012). Strong foundations in phonological awareness, phonemic awareness, and phonics aid in the production of written words, and ultimately, sentences. As their vocabulary expands, children will become more flexible with word choices and more confident with spelling and punctuation. Once children have progressed in their writing to the generative stage (ability to compose phrases and sentences), teachers can help them categorize the types of words that make up sentences—nouns and verbs—and show how these combine to form complete thoughts.

Research by Fearn and Farnan shows that grammar is more effectively learned when taught in the context of writing (2007). While grammatical definitions are important, it is the functionality of grammatical structures that influences writing abilities. Fearn and Farnan conclude, "Grammar knowledge is the elemental foundation for writing. Certainly we should teach grammar, in writing, so learners understand better how the language works, and functionally, so learners can use what they understand about language when they write" (2007, 79). Using mentor texts to identify *nouns* as people, places, or things (and later, ideas) will help children start to recognize the function of nouns as identifiers—they tell about the "thing" in the story. This skill comes more easily to children than recognizing verbs: "Researchers see a robust ability to map nouns to objects . . . but when it comes to mapping verbs to events . . . performance is less robust and more variable" (Anyaso 2013). Children can start by labeling items and objects around them. Then, introduce verbs by asking for an action associated with the noun. "Writers have to be able to rub nouns and verbs together when they write" (Fearn and Farnan 2007, 79), and practices such as these will make the writing more descriptive, expressive, and complex.

When these foundations have been laid, writing instruction in elementary grades can focus on the development and polishing of skilled writing, concentrating on generating increasingly complex and sophisticated sentences, and interesting, well-organized writing.

Joan Sedita (2019) identifies five strands that contribute to skilled writing:

- **Critical thinking**—Critical thinking and executive functioning, awareness of the writing process, the use of background knowledge
- **Syntax**—How sentences work
- **Text structure**—Types of texts, paragraph structures, organizational patterns, linking and transition words
- **Writing craft**—Word choice, audience, and literary devices
- **Transcription**—Spelling, handwriting, and keyboarding

Effective instruction that supports organization, expression, and proper use of conventions includes the use of mentor texts, embedded writing tasks, and instruction in writing at the sentence level (Hochman and Wexler 2017; Tompkins 2018). Early childhood classrooms provide a prime opportunity to embed writing and the discussion of these strands in fun and engaging ways.

Encouraging Developing Writers

Writing confidently starts with a growth mindset. Children need to be able to use invented spelling, scribbles, and drawings without sanction so that they feel comfortable with writing instruments. Markers, crayons, fingerpaints, stickers, or a touchscreen all offer acceptable forms of writing, and show children that they have the power to symbolically represent their thoughts and ideas. Elizabeth Coates and Andrew Coates note, "Drawing, even at the scribble stage, enables children to enter a realm of fantasy as they become characters from stories or other media outlets, taking the level of their play beyond what is possible in the real world" (2016, 61). Coates and Coates also discuss responding to children's work:

> Taking children's work seriously, whatever the subject or type of activity, is extremely important if they are to feel that their efforts are respected and highly regarded. Communication between adults and children includes listening to what they are saying, respecting their intellectual integrity and reinforcing that scribbling is regarded as an exciting, serious, and stimulating activity. (2016, 80)

There are a variety of ways to teach students new ideas and to incorporate writing into the curriculum. Finding opportunities to weave together writing experiences and text is critical. In addition to teaching writer's craft for its own sake, writing can be used to explain and communicate learning and understanding, and as a response to reading. The more students write, the more skilled they will become in both reading and writing. Here are some characteristics of good writers that can inform instructional considerations for developing strong writers in the early childhood classroom:

- Writers write all the time. The more experience one has writing, the better writer one becomes. Learning to write takes practice and more practice! Provide lots of opportunities for writing at centers, during role-play, and across all content area instruction.

- Writers read a lot. Reading provides a great model for writers as to what the finished product looks like. Students who read, or who are read to, will have a stronger base of knowledge about writing. Keep plenty of books around for children to reference and engage with. You may find them mimicking the style or syntax of a storybook, which is a great way to experiment with sentence-building.

- Writers compose for a variety of purposes. Learning to write in a variety of formats makes for a well-rounded, experienced writer. Writers explore different types of writing formats, so provide plenty of instruments for young writers to explore.

- Writers think writing is fun! They have lots of ideas and know how to discern the most important things they want to write. They can use tools to help them organize their thinking, and they have strategies to help them when they feel stuck.

- Writers read their work aloud. Getting a response from classmates or an audience validates the writer's ideas and encourages them to keep writing.

The strategies that follow are designed to support the development of writers. They provide flexible, generic structures, processes, and procedures intended to become a regular part of your writing instruction and writing routines.

Print-Rich Environment

Objectives

- Develop an understanding that print has meaning.
- Use a combination of drawing, dictating, and writing to communicate ideas.

Background Information

Print-Rich Environments provide access to a range of materials, including environmental print, classroom libraries, a writing center, and writing materials throughout the classroom. A Print-Rich Environment provides opportunities for children to develop an understanding that print has purpose and meaning (conceptual knowledge), to use a variety of tools to explore and practice writing (procedural knowledge), and to create their own meaningful writing to share their ideas (generative writing).

Materials

- varies depending on area of classroom (see below)

Process

Create a Print-Rich Environment by integrating the following types of materials throughout the classroom.

- **Labels**. Label different areas of the room, objects, contents of shelves and containers, children's cubbies, etc.

- **Charts**. Post things like a class list, a birthday chart, lunch menus, a helpers chart, a calendar, and the schedule. Provide children with a variety of ways to see their names in print.

- **Writing Products**. Display shared-writing charts, anchor charts, word walls, student journals, and so on.

- **Writing Center**. Include a table and chairs, and a variety of writing materials such as paper of different sizes, shapes, and colors, notepads, notebooks, sticky notes, pencils, markers, crayons, envelopes, clipboards, individual whiteboards, and an alphabet chart. Display words related to thematic or topical units the class is studying.

- **Classroom Library**. Offer picture books, informational books, decodable texts, Big Books, magazines, and comic books. Provide comfortable seating in the form of rugs, pillows, beanbag chairs, and so on.

- **Other Centers (art, dramatic play, science, social studies, etc.).** Offer books and other print materials related to the topic or purpose of the center, display related words, and include directions for using the center. Provide paper, markers, pencils, clipboards, and notepads, and take time to talk with children about how writing relates to the center. For example, scientists make notes about what they observe; servers take orders from customers who read menus; people write grocery shopping lists; and so on.

Ensure that materials can be accessed by children on their own, and whenever possible, display items such as charts at students' eye level to encourage interaction with the items. Draw students' attention to print by interacting with it and pointing to it as you read the words. Draw attention to different ways students use the materials throughout the room. Plan to replace materials periodically to refresh and vary the environment.

Differentiation

Some students will benefit from being individually prompted to use specific materials. Invite students to participate in creating directions for class processes or signs for areas of the classroom. For example, if children need reminders to put books away in the library, have them create signs with one or two reminders using text (and pictures too, if needed). Or have them dictate the reminders while you record them. Allow children to help determine where and how the sign should be displayed.

Multisensory Letter Formation Practice

Objective

- Recognize and name uppercase and lowercase letters.

Background Information

Many young students are not yet ready to begin formal instruction with penmanship; however, multimodal writing activities can still be used to help them practice letter recognition and to prepare them for when more formal penmanship instruction begins. Research suggests that as students form letters while handwriting, neural pathways linked to strong reading skills are being developed (James and Berninger 2019). Writing letters also assists students in learning to recognize letters.

Materials

- varies by activity (see list below)

Process

Students can practice letter formation in a variety of multisensory ways. Although students are not using writing utensils for these activities, watch for correct letter formation and provide support as needed to build good habits. Once students can consistently form letters correctly, place these materials in centers and allow students to use them independently.

- **Skywriting:** Have each student extend the arm of their dominant hand out in front of them and use their index finger to form the letter "in the sky" as you provide the verbal pathway for the letter formation.

- **Gel Bag:** Place a small amount of colored hair gel in well-sealed resealable bags. Have students lay the bags on a flat surface and use their index fingers to form letters by pushing the gel around in the bags.

- **Sand/Salt Trays:** Cover the surface of a plastic plate, pie tin, or other shallow container with sand or salt. Students use their index fingers or the ends of unsharpened pencils to form letters in the sand. Shallow plastic containers or pencil boxes with snap-on lids make storage easy.

- **Shaving Cream:** Spray a small amount of shaving cream on students' desks or in shallow containers such as a plastic plate or pie tin. Have students use the palms of their hands to spread the shaving cream flat. Then, have them use their index fingers to practice letter formation. Provide washable gloves for children who might not want to touch the shaving cream.

- **Finger Trace:** Copy the *Large Uppercase Letter Cards* and *Large Lowercase Letter Cards* (pages 68–77) on cardstock. Trace the shape of each letter with white glue and allow the glue to dry. Have students use their index fingers to trace the shapes of the letters by following the lines of dried glue. To add texture to the letters, sprinkle sand on the glue and allow it to dry.

- **Bendable Material:** Have students form letters using Wikki Stix®, yarn, modeling dough, or chenille stems. Students can form the letters on their own. Or, copy *Large Uppercase Letter Cards* and *Large Lowercase Letter Cards* (pages 68–77) on cardstock and cut out and laminate the cards. Have students lay the bendable materials on top of the letters.

- **Textured Surface:** Cut plastic canvas, sandpaper, scrapbooking paper, or any other type of textured, flat material into 4-inch x 8-inch pieces (one for each student). Students can use their index fingers to practice letter formation on the textured surface.

Differentiation

During the Lesson: Place your hand on top of the hand of a student struggling to form letters and assist them by gently moving their hand with yours.

After the Lesson: When students have begun using writing utensils, put a sheet of paper on top of a textured surface and have them use crayons to write the letter.

Name Writing

Objectives

- Develop an understanding that print has meaning.
- Use a combination of drawing, dictating, and writing to communicate ideas.

Background Information

Meaningful writing opportunities are motivating and help writing make sense to children (Gerde, Bingham, and Wasik 2012). Names are highly meaningful and are often the first word children learn to write. Name Writing supports phonological awareness, letter knowledge, and print concepts (Blair and Savage 2006; Byington and Kim 2017). The early childhood classroom provides many opportunities for children to write their names in meaningful situations, strengthening children's understanding of the connections between oral language and written words.

Materials

- varies depending on the activity (see below)

Process

Provide children with opportunities to write, or attempt to write, their names each day.

- Have children sign in for attendance. This can be done on a whiteboard or a sign-in sheet, with parents supporting children as needed. Another method is to create a sign-in sheet for each child (see the example on the right). Then, each day, the child writes their name to sign in (Sanders 2011).

- Provide opportunities for children to "sign up," for example, for a helper task, to use a computer, have a turn at a busy center, and so on.

Name	Mia
Monday	
Tuesday	
Wednesday	
Thursday	
Friday	

- Ask a daily question that allows children to respond by writing their names. For example, write, "Which do you prefer—dogs or cats?" and place a picture of a dog on the left side and a cat on the right side. Children answer by writing their names under their choice. Or children write their names on sticky notes and place them under their choice.

- Invite children to vote for their choices. For example, place book titles or pictures of the front covers on two shoe boxes. Ask, "What book should we read first?" Children write their names on slips of paper and place them in the box of their choice.

- Have children sign their artwork.

- Provide dramatic play activities in which children write names (e.g., signing for a package, sign in at a doctor's office).

Differentiation

Be supportive of children's attempts to write their names; for some, writing the first letter of their names is an accomplishment. In addition to adults in the room supporting children, peer helpers can also aid in name writing. Provide children with models of their names, and allow them to practice using a variety of materials (see Multisensory Letter Formation Practice on page 141).

Morning Message

Objectives

- Develop an understanding that print has meaning.
- Demonstrate an awareness of concepts of print.
- Use a combination of drawing, dictating, and writing to communicate ideas.

Background Information

The Morning Message is widely used in early childhood classrooms. Teachers often create the message in advance; however, cocreating it with children allows teachers to explicitly model the thinking process that occurs as they compose sentences and translate speech into print (Cabell, Tortorelli, and Gerde 2013). The Morning Message also supports understandings such as phonemic awareness, the alphabetic principle, and concepts of print in an engaging way for young children. The process described here incorporates several guidelines recommended by Barbara Wasik and Annemarie Hindman (2011).

Materials

- chart paper and markers

Process

1. Prepare for the Morning Message by considering the day's schedule and a topic or theme currently being studied.

2. Construct the message in front of the children. Think aloud about how you decide what you want the message to say, making connections to a topic being studied, events that have occurred or will be occurring, and so on. Include key vocabulary (at least one word) related to the topic.

3. As you write, continue to think aloud as you identify letters you are writing, and after writing a word, identify the word. Describe mechanics such as capitalizing the first word of a sentence and using ending punctuation.

4. At times, invite children to contribute to the message. Write their contributions on the chart paper, expanding them if needed. This ensures that the message models correct grammar, letter formation, word spacing, and spelling.

5. Use the Morning Message to support students' learning about a specific letter, phonics pattern, word, or concept. Underline the letter, phonics pattern, or word each time it is written, or you can have children come up and underline it. Encourage the class to skywrite the letter or pattern.

6. Encourage conversation by asking questions about the ideas in the message.

7. Refer back to the Morning Message throughout the day, connecting to vocabulary, letter learning, concepts of print, and so on.

Differentiation

For younger learners, or at the beginning of the year, aim for one or two brief sentences with about six words. As children develop (or for older children), increase the sentence and message length. The message can be used in large groups in the morning to focus on big ideas and can be used again in small groups to focus on letter knowledge and print concepts.

Picture Word Chart

Objectives

- Expand knowledge and use of a wide variety of words.
- Use words and phrases acquired through conversations, reading and being read to, and responding to texts.
- Use a combination of drawing, dictating, and writing to communicate ideas.

Background Information

This strategy supports oral language skills and vocabulary development that in turn support composing written pieces. It is effective with young learners, both native English speakers and English language learners. The teacher shares a picture that includes familiar items and engages children in identifying the items, labeling them, and discussing and writing about the picture. Through this process students "witness the transformation from oral to written expression" (Calhoun 1999, 25) as they connect an object in the picture with a spoken word, and then with a printed word. This strategy is a shortened version of the Picture Word Inductive Model (Calhoun 1999).

Materials

- picture with familiar objects or scenes
- sticky notes

Process

1. Choose a picture that can generate many words related to a current topic of study.

2. Display the picture on chart paper, leaving a border of white space around the picture for labeling objects. Or, if you are using a picture from an item such as a Big Book, you can use sticky notes to label objects in the picture.

3. Share the picture with students. Tell students that you are going to "shake out" all of the words from this picture. Ask, "What do you see?"

4. After a student names an object, label it by drawing a line from the object and writing the word. Spell the word aloud as you write it. When you are finished, have students echo you as you say and spell the word again.

5. Continue the process of identifying and labeling objects in the picture.

6. Review the chart, pointing to each word and reading it aloud together, while tracing the line to the object. Tell the students you will be using the chart again tomorrow.

7. The next day, review the chart by pointing to the words and having students echo read them after you.

8. Ask who has something they would like to say about the picture. Then help children construct sentences about it. Some children may provide a complete sentence. Others may share a word or two; help those children expand their thoughts as needed.

9. Record the sentences, reading each word aloud and having children read the word after you. Continue this process to record several sentences. Then reread all the sentences and have the children echo read them.

Differentiation

Ask questions such as, "What is happening in this picture? Can you describe the ___?" This elicits more information and supports students as they describe the picture. The Picture Word Chart can support more in-depth word study when students are ready. Invite students to find ways the words are alike, for example, common beginning letters, rhyming words, and so on. Choose several of the words based on phonetic targets and create a set of vocabulary cards for each student to use for other reading and writing activities.

Picture Word Chart Example

Experience, Talk, Write

Objectives

- Develop an understanding that print has meaning.
- Demonstrate an awareness of concepts of print.
- Use a combination of drawing, dictating, and writing to communicate ideas.

Background Information

By the end of kindergarten, children are expected to be familiar with three basic genres—opinion writing (a precursor to persuasive writing), informational writing, and narrative writing. In all genres of writing, children should be able to "construct real meaning" (Hawkins et al. 2008, 10). The classroom and children's everyday lives are filled with experiences that are a source for children's oral language development and putting their ideas on paper. The steps below are based on a process for writing with young children described by Timothy Shanahan (2018a) and can be used to develop familiarity with writing in different genres.

Materials

- chart paper

Procedure

1. Provide students with a shared experience based on the targeted genre of writing. This could be a science exploration, a cooking activity, a music experience, a visit to the school library, etc.

2. After the experience, have a class discussion. Prompt the children to talk about the experience. Ask questions to draw out various aspects. If appropriate, introduce signal words into the conversation, e.g., *first*, *next*, *last*.

3. Tell the class that you are going to write a story about the shared experience. Ask who has something that they would like to say about the experience. Then help children construct sentences about it. Some children may provide a complete sentence. Others may share a word or two; help those children expand their thoughts as needed.

4. Record the sentences, reading each word as you write it. Continue until you have several sentences. Then read all the sentences aloud, having the children echo read them.

5. Regularly repeat the process of having a shared experience, talking about it, and writing about it with the whole class.

6. When students are comfortable with the process, conduct the discussion and writing steps in small groups so more children can contribute to the story.

Differentiation

This process can be adapted to include interactive writing, where the teacher "shares the pen" with students, which helps students see themselves as writers. Students can write either a single letter or a word with the teacher's guidance. One strategy is to invite students up to write the first letter of a word that starts with the same first letter as their name. Support students who need help forming the letter by placing your hand over theirs and guiding it. Limit this to a few students each time, and engage the rest of the class by having them write the letter or word in the air.

Journal Writing

Objectives

- Develop an understanding that print has meaning.
- Demonstrate an awareness of concepts of print.
- Use a combination of drawing, dictating, and writing to communicate ideas.

Background Information

Journal Writing is an effective way to ensure that students write every day. It can begin at the start of a school year and go through the full year, and can be used to promote the alphabetic principle, letter knowledge, writing fluency, and writing mechanics.

Materials

- journals made with several sheets of *Journal Paper* (see pages 153 and 154) bound together; one for each child

Procedure

1. Introduce the writing journals to the students and explain that they are going to draw and write in their journals every day.

2. Provide prompts or topics that allow children to draw/write about themselves, their families, current happenings in the classroom, or a current topic of study. For example, the topic could be *bugs*. Ask students to draw a picture related to the topic.

3. Explain that they are going to write about the topic. Accommodate students' varying writing abilities by having them write one or more words about the topic, or have an adult (teacher, paraprofessional, or parent volunteer) take dictation and write for them.

4. Once students become familiar with the process of drawing and writing in their journals each day, which may take six to eight weeks, you can allow them to choose their own topics to draw and write about. Support children in choosing their own topics by working together to create a topic idea list and displaying it. Or, collect picture cards and place them in an "Ideas" container children can access. Show children how to choose a card from the container for a topic.

5. After you have provided explicit instruction on conventions of writing, such as letter formation, punctuation, spacing between words, and so on, encourage students to include those conventions in their writing.

Differentiation

Support students based on their writing level. Cabell, Tortorelli, and Gerde (2013) suggest the following prompts for students at different levels of development:

- **Drawing/scribbling:** Ask children to tell you about their drawings, and write their words.

- **Letters and letter-like forms:** Ask children what they want to write. Then ask what beginning sounds (letters) they hear and have them write those letters.

- **Salient and beginning sounds:** Ask children to say what they want to write. Have the child identify the initial sound, then say the word again and identify the ending sound. Enunciate syllables and ending sounds to help children hear them.

- **Beginning and ending sounds:** Ask children to add details to their pictures. Then have children tell you about the details and write about them. Support children in stretching out the sounds in words.

When students are ready to work with sentence frames, periodically use them for daily journal prompts (sample suggestions below).

This is my ___.	I like to ___.
I love my ___.	Here is a ___.
We went to ___.	I can ___.
I want to ___.	My favorite food is ___.

Name _____

_____

_____

_____

_____

_____

_____

Name

Predictable Sentences

Objectives

- Demonstrate an awareness of concepts of print.
- Use a combination of drawing, dictating, and writing to communicate ideas.

Background Information

Predictable Sentences support young writers by providing a scaffold for sentence construction, word spacing, punctuation, and spelling. Teachers present a sentence frame based on a current topic of interest or study, and children provide words to complete the sentence frame. The sentences are initially written on a chart; as students are ready, the teacher can gradually release more responsibility to them for writing the sentences independently in their writing journals (Collier 2022).

Materials

- chart paper
- sentence frame

Procedure

1. Choose a topic and write a corresponding sentence frame. This can be based on a current thematic unit, and/or it can focus on one or more sight or vocabulary words you want students to work with. See sample sentence frames on page 157.

2. Display the chart paper and write a title, such as *Bugs We See*. Discuss the topic with the students. For example, ask, "What bugs have you seen?"

3. Write the sentence frame on the chart paper and read it aloud. For example, *I can see a ____* . Orally model how to complete the sentence several times. Write an example on the chart and read the sentence; then read it a second time and have students join in with you.

4. Have a student share how they would complete the sentence. Write the sentence on the chart, recording the child's name after the sentence. Repeat the process with the other students. Reread each sentence aloud several times.

5. Engage students in one or more of these activities:
   - Use a special pointer to point to each word in their sentence while the class reads it.
   - Count the number of words in a sentence.
   - Look for specific letters.
   - Identify the shortest word.

6. Distribute story paper to the students. Tell them that they are going to write the sentence on their own. Practice the sentence frame again orally. Have the students write it and add their own word to complete it. Rotate through the classroom, supporting students as they complete their sentences. Students can then illustrate the sentences.

7. As an extension or alternate activity on the following day, cut the chart-paper sentences apart and give them to students to put the words in order to make their sentences. Students can also trade the cut-up sentences with other children and then put their classmates' sentences back together.

Differentiation

Some students will need support writing the sentences on their own. Help these students orally rehearse their sentences, and write each word to complete them. Students who are ready can write additional sentences using the same frame. After students are familiar with using sentence frames, place sentence frames at a writing center for students to use on their own. Swap these out with new frames periodically to correspond with current topics of study.

I can see a fly. (Mila)

I can see a caterpillar. (River)

I can see a grasshopper. (Leo)

I can see a beetle. (Alice)

I can see a ladybug. (Kai)

I can see a butterfly. (Sofia)

I can see a bee. (Amir)

I can see a cricket. (Mateo)

Examples of Sentence Frames

I like to go to the _____.

I like to eat _____.

I play with _____.

I see the _____.

I can help _____.

This is my _____.

We can _____.

All dogs are _____.

I like to play _____.

We saw a _____.

The Big Three

Objectives

- Demonstrate an awareness of concepts of print.
- Use a combination of drawing, dictating, and writing to communicate ideas.

Background Information

Emergent writers who are writing their own sentences need to learn when and how to use word spacing, capitalization, and punctuation. Teachers can explicitly draw attention to examples of their use when reading aloud to students and when engaging in shared writing activities. Cathy Collier refers to these as "the Big 3," and provides a process for explicitly teaching them to students by creating an anchor chart together (2022). After the anchor chart is created, refer to it regularly to remind children to use these conventions.

Materials

- chart paper

Procedure

1. Explain to students that when they write, they can help readers understand what they have written by following three important rules. Tell students that these are the "big three" and write the title *The Big 3* on the chart. Read the title together.

2. Explain that the first thing writers do is start each sentence with a capital letter. Write the number 1 and then write *Start with a capital*.

3. Provide students with examples of sentences that are missing starting capitals or that have capitals in the wrong places. Work together to identify the errors and fix them.

4. The next day, review the first rule. Then introduce the next rule by explaining that we need to be sure there are spaces between words when we write. Write the number 2 and then write *Put in spaces*.

5. Provide students with an example of a simple sentence that has two words that are run together. Work together to identify the words and rewrite the sentence. Repeat this several times.

6. The following day, review the first two rules. Then introduce the third rule by discussing periods, question marks, and exclamation points and what each means. Write the number 3 and then write *End with an end mark*.

7. Provide examples of sentences that are missing periods and work together to add the periods.

8. Review the Big 3 and post the anchor chart in the classroom. Refer to it regularly during writing instruction and practice.

9. When children "finish" a piece of writing, direct their attention to the anchor chart and ask them if they have included the Big 3. Help students identify missing items, and have them make any adjustments needed.

Differentiation

Some students will benefit by using tongue depressors as spacers. Direct individual students to the anchor chart as needed to remind them of these conventions.

REFERENCES

Adams, Marilyn. 2011. "The Relation Between Alphabetic Basics, Word Recognition, and Reading." In *What Research Has to Say About Reading Instruction*, 4th edition, edited by S. Jay Samuels and Alan E. Farstrup, 4–24. Newark, DE: International Reading Association.

Anderson, Richard Chase, and P. David Pearson. 1984. "A Schema-Theoretic View of Basic Processes in Reading Comprehension." In *Handbook of Reading Research*, edited by P. David Pearson, with Rebecca Barr, Michael L. Kamil, and Peter Mosenthal, 255–291. New York: Routledge.

Anderson, Richard C., and William E. Nagy. 1992. "The Vocabulary Conundrum." *American Educator* 16 (4): 14–18, 44–47.

Anyaso, Hilary H. 2013. "Language Acquisition: Nouns Before Verbs?" *ScienceDaily*, March 25, 2013. sciencedaily.com/releases/2013/03/130325184020.htm.

Armbruster, Bonnie B., Fran Lehr, and Jean Osborn. 2010. *Put Reading First: The Research Building Blocks for Teaching Children to Read: Kindergarten Through Grade 3*. 3rd edition. National Institute for Literacy.

BabySparks. 2020. "How Signs and Symbols Support Language Development." *BabySparks*, May 11, 2020. babysparks.com/2020/05/11/how-signs-symbols-support-language-development/.

Baker, Linda, and Ann L. Brown. 1984. "Metacognitive Skills and Reading." In *Handbook of Reading Research*, edited by P. David. Pearson, Michael L. Kamil, Peter B. Mosenthal, and Rebecca Barr, 353–394. New York: Longman.

Barnes, Douglas, and Frankie Todd. 1995. *Communication and Learning Revisited*. Portsmouth, NH: Heinemann.

Beck, Isabel L., Margaret G. McKeown, and Linda Kucan. 2013. *Bringing Words to Life*. New York: Guilford Press.

Blair, Rebecca, and Robert Savage. 2006. "Name Writing but not Environmental Print Recognition Is Related to Letter-Sound Knowledge and Phonological Awareness in Pre-Readers." *Reading and Writing* 19: 991–1016.

Brown, Carmen S. 2014. "Language and Literacy Development in the Early Years: Foundational Skills that Support Emergent Readers." *The Language and Literacy Spectrum* 24: 35–49.

Brown, Margaret Wise. 1947. *Goodnight Moon*. New York: HarperCollins.

Burchinal, Margaret R., Sarah Krowka, Rebecca Newman-Gonchar, Madhavi Jayanthi, Russell Gersten, Samantha Wavell, Julia Lyskawa et al. 2022. "Preparing Young Children for School." *What Works Clearinghouse 2022009*. Washington, DC: National Center for Education Evaluation and Regional Assistance (NCEE), Institute of Education Sciences, U.S. Department of Education. whatworks.ed.gov.

Byington, Teresa A., and YaeBin Kim. 2017. "Promoting Preschoolers' Emergent Writing." *Young Children* 72 (5) 5: 74–82. naeyc.org/resources/pubs/yc/nov2017/emergent-writing.

Cabell, Sonia Q., and HyeJin Hwang. 2020. "Building Content Knowledge to Boost Comprehension in the Primary Grades." *Reading Research Quarterly* 55 (S1): S99– S107. doi.org/10.1002/rrq.338.

Cabell, Sonia Q., Laura S. Tortorelli, and Hope K. Gerde. 2013. "How Do I Write…? Scaffolding Preschoolers' Early Writing Skills." *The Reading Teacher* 66 (8): 650–659. doi.org/10.1002/trtr.1173.

Calhoun, Emily F. 1999. *Teaching Beginning Reading and Writing with the Picture Word Inductive Model.* Alexandria, VA: ASCD.

Cervetti, Gina N., Tanya S. Wright, and HyeJin Hwang. 2016. "Conceptual Coherence, Comprehension, and Vocabulary Acquisition: A Knowledge Effect?" *Reading and Writing* 29 (4): 761–779. doi.org/10.1007/ 1145-016-9628-x.

Coates, Elizabeth, and Andrew Coates. 2016. "The Essential Role of Scribbling in the Imaginative and Cognitive Development of Young Children." *Journal of Early Childhood Literacy* 16 (1): 60–83. doi.org/10.1177/1468798415577871.

Collier, Cathy. 2022. *The Road to Independent Reading and Writing.* Huntington Beach, CA: Shell Education.

Cromley, Jennifer G., and Roger Azevedo. 2007. "Testing and Refining the Direct and Inferential Mediation Model of Reading Comprehension." *Journal of Educational Psychology* 99 (2): 311–325. doi.org/10.1037/0022-0663.99.2.311.

Dewitz, Peter, Michael Graves, Bonnie Graves, and Connie Juel. 2020. *Teaching Reading in the 21st Century: Motivating All Learners.* 6th edition. Saddle River, NJ: Pearson.

Dooley, Caitlin M. 2010. "Young Children's Approaches to Books: The Emergence of Comprehension." *The Reading Teacher* 64 (2): 120–130.

———. 2011. "The Emergence of Comprehension: A Decade of Research 2000–2010." *International Electronic Journal of Elementary Education* 4 (1): 169–184. files.eric.ed.gov/fulltext/EJ1068604.pdf.

Duke, Nell K., and Kelly B. Cartwright. 2021. "The Science of Reading Progresses: Communicating Advances Beyond the Simple View of Reading." *Reading Research Quarterly* (Special Issue) 56 (S1): S25–S44. doi.org/10.1002/rrq.411.

Duke, Nell K., and Heidi Anne E. Mesmer. 2018. "Phonics Faux Pas: Avoiding Instructional Missteps in Teaching Letter-Sound Relationships." *American Educator* 42 (4): 12–16. aft. org/ae/winter2018-2019/duke_mesmer.

Duke, Nell K., and P. David Pearson. 2002. "Effective Practices for Developing Reading Comprehension." In *What Research Has to Say About Reading Instruction*, edited by Alan E. Farstrup and S. Jay Samuels, 3rd edition, 205–242. Newark, DE: International Reading Association.

Duke, Nell K., Alessandra E. Ward, and P. David Pearson. 2021. "The Science of Reading Comprehension Instruction." *The Reading Teacher* 74 (6): 663–672. doi.org/10.1002/trtr.1993.

Dunlap, Carmen Zuñiga, and Evelyn Marino Weisman. 2006. *Helping English Language Learners Succeed.* Huntington Beach, CA: Shell Education.

Durkin, Dolores. 1978. "What Classroom Observations Reveal About Reading Comprehension." *Reading Research Quarterly* 14 (4): 481–553. Newark, DE: International Reading Association.

Ehri, Linnea C. 1987. "Learning to Read and Spell Words." *Journal of Reading Behavior* 19 (1): 5–31.

———. 1992. "Reconceptualizing the Development of Sight Word Reading and Its Relationship to Recoding." In *Reading Acquisition*, edited by Philip B. Gough, Linnea C. Ehri, and Rebecca Treiman, 107–143. Hillsdale, NJ: Erlbaum.

———. 1995. "Phases of Development in Learning to Read Words by Sight." *Journal of Research in Reading* 18 (2): 116–125. doi.org/10.1111/j.1467-9817.1995.tb00077.x.

———. 1998. "Grapheme-Phoneme Knowledge Is Essential for Learning to Read Words in English." In *Word Recognition in Beginning Literacy,* edited by Jamie L. Metsala and Linnea C. Ehri, 3–40. Mahwah, NJ: Erlbaum.

———. 2005. "Learning to Read Words: Theory, Findings and Issues." *Scientific Studies of Reading* 9 (2): 167–188.

———. 2005a. "Development of Sight Word Reading: Phases and Findings." In *The Science of Reading: A Handbook,* edited by M. J. Snowling and C. Hulme, 135–154. Malden, MA: Blackwell.

———. 2014. "Orthographic Mapping in the Acquisition of Sight Word Reading, Spelling Memory, and Vocabulary Learning." *Scientific Studies of Reading* 18 (1): 5–21. doi.org/10.1080/10888438.2013.819356.

———. 2017. "Orthographic Mapping and Literacy Development Revisited." In *Theories of Reading Development*, edited by Kate Cain, Donald L. Compton, and Rauno K. Parrila, 127–146. Amsterdam, The Netherlands: John Benjamins.

———. 2020. "The Science of Learning to Read Words: A Case for Systematic Reading Instruction." *Reading Research Quarterly* 55: S45–S60.

Ehri, Linnea C., Simone R. Nunes, Steven A. Stahl, and Dale M. Willows. 2001. "Systematic Phonics Instruction Helps Students Learn to Read: Evidence from the National Reading Panel's Meta-Analysis." *Review of Educational Research* 71 (3): 393–447. doi.org/10.3102/00346543071003393.

Elleman, Amy M., and Eric L. Oslund. 2019. "Reading Comprehension Research: Implications for Practice and Policy." *Policy Insights from the Behavioral and Brain Sciences* 6 (1): 3–11. doi.org/10.1177/2372732218816339.

Fearn, Leif, and Nancy Farnan. 2007. "When Is a Verb? Using Functional Grammar to Teach Writing." *Journal of Basic Writing* 26 (1): 63–87.

Fitzgerald, Jill, Jeff Elmore, Jackie Eunjung Relyea, and A. Jackson Stenner. 2020. "Domain-Specific Academic Vocabulary Network Development in Elementary Grades Core Disciplinary Textbooks." *Journal of Educational Psychology 112* (5): 855–879.

Foorman, B., N. Beyler, K. Borradaile, M. Coyne, C. A. Denton, J. Dimino, J. Furgeson, L. Hayes, J. Henke, L. Justice, B. Keating, W. Lewis, S. Sattar, A. Streke, R. Wagner, and S. Wissel. 2016. *Foundational Skills to Support Reading for Understanding in Kindergarten Through 3rd Grade*. NCEE 2016-4008. Washington, DC: U.S. Department of Education.

Ganea, Patricia A., Melissa Allen, Lucas Butler, Susan Carey, and Judy S. DeLoache. 2009. "Toddlers' Referential Understanding of Pictures." *Journal of Experimental Child Psychology* 104 (3): 283–295. doi.org/10.1016/j.jecp.2009.05.008.

Gerde, Hope K., Gary E. Bingham, and Barbara A. Wasik. 2012. "Writing in Early Childhood Classrooms: Guidance for Best Practices." *Early Childhood Education Journal* 40: 351–359. doi.org/10.1007/ 0643-012-0531-z.

Gough, Philip B., Connie Juel, and D. Roper-Schneider. 1983. "Code and Cipher: A Two-Stage Conception of Initial Reading Acquisition." In *Searches for Meaning in Reading/ Language Processing and Instruction*, edited by J. A. Niles and L. A. Harris, 207–211. Rochester, NY: National Reading Conference.

Gough, Philip B., and William E. Tunmer. 1986. "Decoding, Reading, and Reading Disability." *Remedial and Special Education* 7 (1): 6–10.

Gourgey, Annette F. 1998. "Metacognition in Basic Skills Instruction." *Instructional Science* 26 (1/2): 81–96. Philadelphia: Kluwer Academic Publishers. doi. org/10.1023/a:1003092414893.

Graham, Steve. 2020. "The Sciences of Reading and Writing Must Become More Fully Integrated." *Reading Research Quarterly* 55 (S1): S35–S44. doi.org/10.1002/rrq.332.

Graham, Steve, Debra McKeown, Sharlene Kiuhara, and Karen R. Harris. 2012. "A Meta-Analysis of Writing Instruction for Students in the Elementary Grades." *Journal of Educational Psychology* 104 (4): 879–896. doi.org/10.1037/a0029185.

Greenwood, Scott C., and Kevin Flanigan. 2007. "Overlapping Vocabulary and Comprehension: Context Clues Complement Semantic Gradients." *The Reading Teacher* 61 (3): 249–254.

Hacker, Douglas J., John Dunlosky, and Arthur C. Graesser. 1998. *Metacognition in Educational Theory and Practice*. Mahwah, NJ: Erlbaum.

Hall, Kendra M., and Brenda L. Sabey. 2007. "Focus on the Facts: Using Informational Texts Effectively in Early Elementary Classrooms." *Early Childhood Education Journal* 35 (3): 261–268.

Halliday, M. A. K. 1975. *Learning How to Mean: Explorations in the Development of Language*. London: Edward Arnold.

Halliday, Michael A. 2004. *The Language of Early Childhood*. New York: Continuum.

Hattie, John. 2009. *Visible Learning: A Synthesis of Over 800 Meta-Analyses Relating to Achievement*. New York: Routledge.

Hawkins, Joey, Eloise Ginty, Karen LeClaire Kurzman, Diana Leddy, and Jane Miller. 2008. *Writing for Understanding*. South Strafford, VT: Vermont Writing Collaborative.

Hiebert, Elfrieda H., P. David Pearson, Barbara M. Taylor, Virginia Richardson, and Scott G. Paris. 1998. *Every Child a Reader: Applying Reading Research in the Classroom*. Ann Arbor: CIERA/University of Michigan.

Hochman, Judith C., and Natalie Wexler. 2017. "One Sentence at a Time: The Need for Explicit Instruction in Teaching Students to Write Well." *American Educator,* Summer 2017. American Federation of Teachers. aft.org/ae/summer2017/hochman-wexler.

Hollie, Sharroky. 2018. *Culturally and Linguistically Responsive Teaching and Learning, Second Edition*. Huntington Beach, CA: Shell Education.

Hoover, Wesley A., and Philip B. Gough. 1990. "The Simple View of Reading." *Reading and Writing: An Interdisciplinary Journal* 2 (2): 127–160. doi.org/10.1007/BF00401799.

Hoover, Wesley A., and William E. Tunmer. 2018. "The Simple View of Reading: Three Assessments of Its Adequacy." *Remedial and Special Education* 39 (5): 304–312. doi.org/10.1177/0741932518773154.

———. 2020. *The Cognitive Foundations of Reading and Its Acquisition: A Framework with Applications Connecting Teaching and Learning (Literacy Studies)*. London: Springer.

———. 2022. "The Primacy of Science in Communicating Advances in the Science of Reading." *Reading Research Quarterly* (57) 2: 399–408. doi.org/10.1002/rrq.446.

Horton, Phillip B., Andrew A. McConney, Michael Gallo, Amanda L. Woods, Gary J. Senn, and Denis Hamelin. 1993. "An Investigation of the Effectiveness of Concept Mapping as an Instructional Tool." *Science Education* 77 (1): 95–111. doi.org/10.1002/sce.3730770107.

Hulit, Lloyd M., Merle R. Howard, and Kathleen R. Fahey. 2018. *Born to Talk: An Introduction to Speech and Language Development*. 7th edition. Boston, MA: Allyn and Bacon.

James, Karin, and Virginia Berninger. 2019. "Brain Research Shows Why Handwriting Should be Taught in the Computer Age." *Learning Difficulties Australia Bulletin* 51 (1): 25–30.

Jump, Jennifer, and Robin D. Johnson. 2023. *What the Science of Reading Says about Word Recognition*. Huntington Beach, CA: Shell Education.

Jump, Jennifer, and Kathleen Kopp. 2023. *What the Science of Reading Says about Reading Comprehension and Content Knowledge*. Huntington Beach, CA: Shell Education.

Jump, Jennifer, and Hillary Wolfe. 2023. *What the Science of Reading Says about Writing.* Huntington Beach, CA: Shell Education.

Justice, Laura M., and Amy E. Sofka. 2010. *Engaging Children with Print: Building Early Literacy Skills Through Quality Read-Alouds.* New York: Guilford Publications.

Keesey, Susan, Moira Konrad, and Laurice M. Joseph. 2015. "Word Boxes Improve Phonemic Awareness, Letter–Sound Correspondences, and Spelling Skills of At-Risk Kindergartners." *Remedial and Special Education* 36 (3): 167–180.

Kilpatrick, David A. 2015. *Essentials of Assessing, Preventing, and Overcoming Reading Difficulties.* Hoboken, NJ: Wiley.

———. 2016. *Equipped for Reading Success: A Comprehensive, Step-by-Step Program for Developing Phonemic Awareness and Fluent Word Recognition.* Syracuse, New York: Casey and Kirsch.

Kim, Young-Suk, Stephanie Al Otaiba, Cynthia Puranik, Jessica Sidler Folsom, Luana Greulich, and Richard K. Wagner. 2011. "Componential Skills of Beginning Writing: An Exploratory Study." *National Institutes of Health Public Access*: 1–22. ncbi.nlm.nih.gov/pmc/articles/PMC3261783/.

Lapp, Diane, James Flood, and Nancy Farnan, eds. 2008. *Content Area Reading and Learning: Instructional Strategies.* 3rd edition. Boston: Allyn and Bacon.

Lehr, Fran, Jean Osborn, and Elfrieda H. Hiebert. 2004. *Research-Based Practices in Early Reading Series: A Focus on Vocabulary.* Honolulu: Pacific Resources for Education and Learning.

Massey, Susan L. 2014. "Making the Case for Using Informational Text in Preschool Classrooms." *Creative Education* 5 (6): 396–401. doi.org/10.4236/ce.2014.56049.

Moats, Louisa C. 2020a. "Teaching Reading Is Rocket Science." *American Educator*, Summer 2020. aft.org/ae/summer2020/moats.

Moats, Louisa Cook. 2020b. *Speech to Print: Language Essentials for Teachers.* Baltimore: Paul H. Brookes.

Morris, Darrell. 1993. "The Relationship Between Children's Concept of Word in Text and Phoneme Awareness in Learning to Read: A Longitudinal Study." *Research in the Teaching of English* 27 (2):133–154.

Morrow, Lesley Mandel. 2003. "Motivating Lifelong Voluntary Readers." In *Handbook of Research on Teaching the English Language Arts*, edited by James Flood, Diane Lapp, James R. Squire, and Julie M. Jenson, 857–67. Mahwah, NJ: Erlbaum.

National Early Literacy Panel. 2008. *Developing Early Literacy: Report of the National Early Literacy Panel: A Scientific Synthesis of Early Literacy Development and Implications for Intervention.* Jessup, MD: National Institute for Literacy with National Center for Family Literacy.

National Governors Association Center for Best Practices and Council of Chief State School Officers. 2010. "Writing Standards K–5: Kindergarten Writing." *Common Core State Standards for English Language Arts and Literacy in History/Social Studies, Science, and Technical Subjects.* Washington, DC: Authors.

National Reading Panel (U.S.) and National Institute of Child Health and Human Development (U.S.). 2000. *Report of the National Reading Panel: Teaching Children to Read: An Evidence-based Assessment of the Scientific Research Literature on Reading and Its Implications for Reading Instructio*n. Bethesda: U.S. Dept. of Health and Human Services, Public Health Service, National Institutes of Health, National Institute of Child Health and Human Development.

Neuman, Susan B., Tanya Kaefer, and Ashley Pinkham. 2014. "Building Background Knowledge." *The Reading Teacher* 68 (2): 145–148.

Nolen, Susan B. 2007. "Young Children's Motivation to Read and Write: Development in Social Contexts." *Cognition and Instruction* 25 (2–3): 219–270.

Palincsar, Annemarie Sullivan, and Deborah A. Brown. 1987. "Enhancing Instructional Time Through Attention to Metacognition." *Journal of Learning Disabilities* 20 (2): 66–75. Thousand Oaks, CA: SAGE Publications. doi.org/10.1177/002221948702000201.

Perfetti, Charles, and Joseph Stafura. 2013. "Word Knowledge in a Theory of Reading Comprehension." *Scientific Studies of Reading* 18 (1): 22–37. doi.org/10.1080/10888438.2013.827687.

Pressley, Michael, and Peter Afflerbach. 1995. *Verbal Protocols of Reading: The Nature of Constructively Responsive Reading.* New York: Routledge.

Pressley, Michael, Sara E. Dolezal, Lisa M. Raphael, Lindsey Mohan, Alysia D. Roehrig, and Kristen Bogner. 2003. *Motivating Primary-Grade Students.* New York: Guilford.

Puranik, Cynthia S., and Christopher J. Lonigan. 2014. "Emergent Writing in Preschoolers: Preliminary Evidence for a Theoretical Framework." *Reading Research Quarterly* 49 (4): 453–467. doi.org/10.1002/rrq.79.

Rasinski, Timothy, David Paige, Cameron Rains, Fran Stewart, Brenda Julovich, Deb Prenkert, William H. Rupley, and William Dee Nichols. 2017. "Effects of Intensive Fluency Instruction on the Reading Proficiency of Third-Grade Struggling Readers." *Reading & Writing Quarterly* 33 (6): 519–532. doi.org/10.1080/10573569.2016.1250144.

Reutzel, D. Ray. 2015. "Early Literacy Research: Findings Primary-Grade Teachers Will Want to Know." *The Reading Teacher* 69 (1): 14–24. doi.org/10.1002/trtr.1387.

Roberts, Beth. 1992. "The Evolution of the Young Child's Concept of 'Word' as a Unit of Spoken and Written Language." *Reading Research Quarterly* 27 (2):124–138.

Rupley, William H., John W. Logan, and William D. Nichols. 1999. "Vocabulary Instruction in a Balanced Reading Program." *The Reading Teacher* 52 (4): 336–346. Newark, DE: International Reading Association.

Ryder, Randall J., and Michael F. Graves. 2003. *Reading and Learning in Content Areas*. 3rd edition. Hoboken, NJ: John Wiley & Sons.

Sanders, Tami. 2011. "Daily Child Sign-In." *Learning and Teaching Preschoolers* (blog), November 8, 2011. learningandteachingwithpreschoolers.blogspot.com/2011/11/daily-child-sign-in.html.

Scarborough, Hollis S. 2001. "Connecting Early Language and Literacy to Later Reading (Dis)abilities: Evidence, Theory, and Practice." In *Handbook of Early Literacy Research*, edited by Susan B. Neuman and David K. Dickinson, 97–110. New York: Guilford.

Sedita, Joan. 2019. "The Strands That Are Woven into Skilled Writing." Keys to Literacy. keystoliteracy.com/wp-content/uploads/2020/02/The-Strands-That-Are-Woven-Into-Skilled-WritingV2.pdf.

Shanahan, Timothy. 2018a. "How to Teach Writing in Kindergarten." *Reading Rockets: Shanahan on Literacy* (blog), February 21, 2018. readingrockets.org/blogs/shanahan-literacy/how-teach-writing-kindergarten.

———. 2018b. "Synthetic Phonics or Systematic Phonics? What Does Research Really Say?" *Reading Rockets: Shanahan on Literacy* (blog), August 8, 2018. readingrockets.org/blogs/shanahan-literacy/synthetic-phonics-or-systematic-phonics-what-does-research-really-say.

———. 2018c. "Where Questioning Fits in Comprehension Instruction: Skills and Strategies." *Reading Rockets: Shanahan on Literacy* (blog), June 1, 2018. readingrockets.org/blogs/shanahan-literacy/where-questioning-fits-comprehension-instruction-skills-and-strategies.

———. 2021. "What Does It Take to Teach Inferencing?" *Reading Rockets: Shanahan on Literacy* (blog), August 7, 2021. readingrockets.org/blogs/shanahan-literacy/what-does-it-take-teach-inferencing.

Shanahan, Timothy, Kim Callison, Christine Carriere, Nell K. Duke, P. David Pearson, Christopher Schatschneider, and Joseph Torgesen. 2010. *Improving Reading Comprehension in Kindergarten through 3rd Grade: A Practice Guide* (NCEE 2010-4038). Washington, DC: National Center for Education Evaluation and Regional Assistance, Institute of Education Sciences, U.S. Department of Education.

Sinatra, Richard, Vicky Zygouris-Coe, and Sheryl B. Dasinger. 2012. "Preventing a Vocabulary Lag: What Lessons Are Learned from Research." *Reading and Writing Quarterly* 28 (4): 333–357. doi.org/10.1080/10573569.2012.702040.

Smith, Reid, Pamela Snow, Tanya Serry, and Lorraine Hammond. 2021. "The Role of Background Knowledge in Reading Comprehension: A Critical Review." *Reading Psychology* 42 (3): 214–240. doi.org/10.1080/02702711.2021.1888348.

Snow, Catherine E. 2018. "Simple and Not-So-Simple Views of Reading." *Remedial and Special Education* 39 (5): 313–316. doi.org/10.1177/0741932518770288.

Snow, Catherine E., and Connie Juel. 2005. "Teaching Children to Read: What Do We Know about How to Do It?" In *The Science of Reading: A Handbook*, edited by Margaret J. Snowling and Charles Hulme, 501–520. Oxford: Blackwell. doi. org/10.1002/9780470757642.ch26.

Sticht, Thomas G., and James H. James. 1984. "Listening and Reading." In *Handbook of Reading Research*, edited by P. David Pearson, with Rebecca Barr, Michael L. Kamil, and Peter Mosenthal, 293–318. New York: Routledge.

Tomlinson, Carol A. 2014. *The Differentiated Classroom: Responding to the Needs of All Learners*. 2nd edition. Alexandria, VA: ASCD.

Tompkins, Gail. 2018. *Teaching Writing: Balancing Process and Product*. 7th edition. Saddle River, NJ: Pearson.

Wanzek, Jeanne, Elizabeth A. Stevens, Kelly J. Williams, Nancy Scammacca, Sharon Vaugh, and Katherine Sargent. 2018. "Current Evidence on the Effects of Intensive Early Reading Interventions." *Journal of Learning Disabilities* 51 (6): 612–624. doi. org/10.1177/0022219418775110.

Wasik, Barbara A., and Annemarie H. Hindman. 2011. "The Morning Message in Early Childhood Classrooms: Guidelines for Best Practices." *Early Childhood Education Journal* 39: 183–189.

Wasik, Barbara A., and Annemarie H. Hindman. 2020. "Increasing Preschoolers' Vocabulary Development through a Streamlined Teacher Professional Development Intervention." *Early Childhood Research Quarterly* 50 (2020): 101–113.

Wattenberg, Ruth. 2016. "Inside the Common Core Reading Tests: Why the Best Prep Is a Knowledge-Rich Curriculum." *Knowledge Matters*, Issue Brief #7, September 2016, knowledgematterscampaign.org/wp-content/uploads/2016/09/Wattenberg.pdf.

Wilhelm, Jeffrey D., Adam Fachler, and Rachel E. Bear. 2019. *Planning Powerful Instruction, Grades 6-12: Seven Must-Make Moves to Transform How We Teach and How Students Learn*. Thousand Oaks, CA: Corwin.

Willingham, Daniel T. 2006. "How Knowledge Helps: It Speeds and Strengthens Reading Comprehension, Learning—and Thinking." *American Educator,* Spring 2006. American Federation of Teachers. aft.org/periodical/american-educator/spring-2006/how-knowledge-helps.

Wolfersberger, Mary E., D. Ray Reutzel, Richard Sudweeks, and Parker C. Fawson. 2004. "Developing and Validating the Classroom Literacy Environmental Profile (CLEP): A Tool for Examining the 'Print Richness' of Early Childhood and Elementary Classrooms." *Journal of Literacy Research* 36 (2): 211–272.

Yopp, Hallie Kay, and Ruth Helen Yopp. 2022. *Purposeful Play for Early Childhood Phonological Awareness*, 2nd edition. Huntington Beach, CA: Shell Education.

Zavala, Elisavet, and Josh Cuevas. 2019. "Effects of Repeated Reading and Rhyming Poetry on Reading Fluency." *International Journal of Social Sciences and Educational Studies* 6 (2): 64–88. doi.org/10.23918/ijsses.v6i2p64.

Zucker, Tricia A., Allison E. Ward, and Laura M. Justice. 2009. "Print Referencing During Read-Alouds: A Technique for Increasing Emergent Readers' Print Knowledge." *The Reading Teacher* 63 (1): 62–72.

Digital Resources

Accessing the Digital Resources

The digital resources can be downloaded by following these steps:

1. Go to www.tcmpub.com/digital

2. Use the 13-digit ISBN number to redeem the digital resources.

3. Respond to the question using the book.

4. Follow the prompts on the Content Cloud website to sign in or create a new account.

5. The content redeemed will now be on your My Content screen. Click on the product to look through the digital resources. All file resources are available for download. Select files can be previewed, opened, and shared. Any web-based content, such as videos, links, or interactive text, can be viewed and used in the browser but is not available for download.

For questions and assistance with your ISBN redemption, please contact Teacher Created Materials.

> **email:** customerservice@tcmpub.com

> **phone:** 800-858-7339

Contents of the Digital Resources

The digital resources include templates for the classroom resources and student activity pages in this book.